THE SAGA OF A REAL-LIFE BUCCANEER

Captain Bernhard Rogge commanded the ship most feared by the Allies during World War II.

The *Atlantis* was a Nazi raider with no destination and only one mission: to seek and destroy enemy cargo ships on the high seas. The cunning, skill and daring of its crew made it a legend of naval warfare. Here is the story of its incredible voyage, told by the man who outwitted the entire Allied fleet with his single ship.

THE GERMAN RAIDER ATLANTIS
by
Captain Bernhard Rogge
and
Wolfgang Frank

THE BANTAM WAR BOOK SERIES

This is a series of books about a world on fire.

These carefully chosen volumes cover the full dramatic sweep of World War II. Many are eyewitness accounts by the men who fought in this global conflict in which the future of the civilized world hung in balance. Fighter pilots, tank commanders and infantry commanders, among others, recount exploits of individual courage in the midst of the large-scale terrors of war. They present portraits of brave men and true stories of gallantry and cowardice in action, moving sagas of survival and tragedies of untimely death. Some of the stories are told from the enemy viewpoint to give the reader an immediate sense of the incredible life and death struggle of both sides of the battle.

Through these books we begin to discover what it was like to be there, a participant in an epic war for freedom.

Each of the books in the Bantam War Book series contains a dramatic color painting and illustrations specially commissioned for each title to give the reader a deeper understanding of the roles played by the men and machines of World War II.

THE GERMAN RAIDER ATLANTIS

BY CAPTAIN BERNHARD ROGGE AND WOLFGANG FRANK

Translated by Lt.-Cdr. R. O. B. Long, RNVR

THE GERMAN RAIDER ATLANTIS
*A Bantam Book / published by arrangement with the authors
Bantam edition / August 1979*

Drawings by Greg Beecham.

Maps by Benjamin F. Klaessig.

ISBN 0-553-13121-4

Published simultaneously in the United States and Canada

CONTENTS

PART THREE—ROUND THE WORLD
January–November 1941

PART FOUR—HOMEWARD BOUND
November 22, 1941–New Year's Day, 1942

THE GERMAN RAIDER ATLANTIS

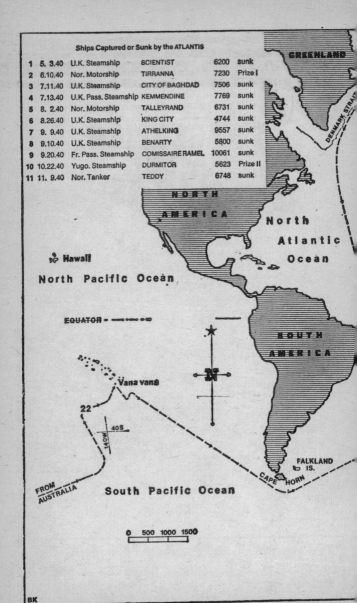

		Ships Captured or Sunk by the ATLANTIS			
1	5. 3.40	U.K. Steamship	SCIENTIST	6200	sunk
2	6.10.40	Nor. Motorship	TIRRANNA	7230	Prize I
3	7.11.40	U.K. Steamship	CITY OF BAGHDAD	7506	sunk
4	7.13.40	U.K. Pass. Steamship	KEMMENDINE	7769	sunk
5	8. 2.40	Nor. Motorship	TALLEYRAND	6731	sunk
6	8.26.40	U.K. Steamship	KING CITY	4744	sunk
7	9. 9.40	U.K. Steamship	ATHELKING	9557	sunk
8	9.10.40	U.K. Steamship	BENARTY	5800	sunk
9	9.20.40	Fr. Pass. Steamship	COMISSAIRE RAMEL	10061	sunk
10	10.22.40	Yugo. Steamship	DURMITOR	5623	Prize II
11	11. 9.40	Nor. Tanker	TEDDY	6748	sunk

GREENLAND

DENMARK STRAIT

NORTH AMERICA

North Atlantic Ocean

Hawaii

North Pacific Ocean

EQUATOR

SOUTH AMERICA

Vana vana

22

40S

140W

FROM AUSTRALIA

South Pacific Ocean

FALKLAND IS.

CAPE HORN

0 500 1000 1500

BK

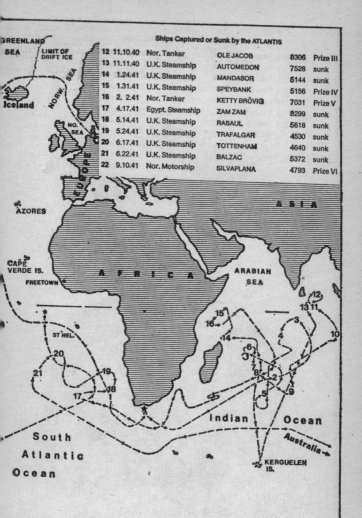

Ships Captured or Sunk by the ATLANTIS

12	11.10.40	Nor. Tanker	OLE JACOB	8306	Prize III
13	11.11.40	U.K. Steamship	AUTOMEDON	7528	sunk
14	1.24.41	U.K. Steamship	MANDASOR	5144	sunk
15	1.31.41	U.K. Steamship	SPEYBANK	5156	Prize IV
16	2. 2.41	Nor. Tanker	KETTY BRÖVIG	7031	Prize V
17	4.17.41	Egypt. Steamship	ZAM ZAM	8299	sunk
18	5.14.41	U.K. Steamship	RABAUL	5618	sunk
19	5.24.41	U.K. Steamship	TRAFALGAR	4530	sunk
20	6.17.41	U.K. Steamship	TOTTENHAM	4640	sunk
21	6.22.41	U.K. Steamship	BALZAC	5372	sunk
22	9.10.41	Nor. Motorship	SILVAPLANA	4793	Prize VI

The voyage of the Raider ATLANTIS
across the "Seven Seas"

⊙ EMBARKATION - MAR. 31 1940   ★ MINE LAYING

Bernhard Rogge

PART ONE
THE ATLANTIC
July 1939–May 1940

1

FITTING OUT

At the end of July, 1939, I took the sailing training ship *Albert Leo Schlageter* with a crew of petty officer cadets on a cruise into the Baltic. It was less than a month since I had come back from a routine cruise to South America, and on returning to Germany I had immediately noticed the tension in the air. People were overwrought by the rumors of war that were everywhere to be heard yet we all felt that a real war would be criminal madness and for this reason alone we were convinced that it could never happen.

Nevertheless before sailing I took the precaution of making some inquiries about my assignment to a command in the unhappy event of hostilities breaking out. The official at the Officers' Appointments Branch looked down his mobilization list and then winked as he said with obvious envy, "*If* anything happens, you've got a plum job. There, read it for yourself!" On the index card was this entry, "Rogge, Bernhard, Commander. War appointment: SHK II, in command."

"The letters SHK stand for Heavy Armed Merchant Cruiser," said the official. "It's the finest job going. *Wolf, Möwe, Seeadler*—commerce raiding, coral beaches and palm trees—you know the form."

The three ships he had mentioned were famous commerce raiders in the First World War. I thanked him warmly and sailed off cheerfully enough with my young crew into the Baltic; yet I grew daily more certain that the parting of the ways was near—not only from my beloved sailing ship with her well-scrubbed

Albert Leo Schlageter

teak decks, her lofty masts and smartly trimmed yards, but from an untroubled and pleasant existence.

I was not really surprised, therefore, to receive an order to break off the cruise and return immediately to Kiel, "because enemy submarines had been sighted in the Baltic"; the date was August 25, 1939. The tension was acute as we speculated on the chances of reaching a peaceful settlement with Poland, but on September 1st the sound of bugles rang out from our wireless loudspeaker followed by the unmistakable voice of the Führer announcing that "as from 6 A.M. we shall return the enemy's fire." England declared war on us two days later and what had been a local punitive police action broadened into a new world conflict.

I immediately got in touch by telephone with the naval authorities at Bremen who were responsible for converting and fitting out the auxiliary cruiser. I received a rather surprising reply to the effect that nothing was known either about my ship or myself and I decided to go to Bremen and find out what had happened. The misunderstanding was soon cleared up and I located the ship and made arrangements to move her into the dockyard. I took care to wear plain clothes, as secrecy was paramount.

Next I visited the newly opened Naval Drafting Office at Bremen, where I was shown a pile of name cards which were intended for issue as personal identity cards to the crew of "Heavy Auxiliary Cruiser II"—as was written in bold letters on each card—yet nobody was supposed to know that such a thing as an armed merchant cruiser even existed! For security reasons the men who held these passes were moved to the barracks of the Petty Officers' Training School at Bremerhaven, where we gradually assembled a carefully selected crew under the noncommittal designation of "Ship 16." I took up my quarters at the Hotel Columbus in Bremen and here I was joined by the twenty-odd officers who were to serve under me. The sooner they got to know me and each other, the better; only by making close personal contact with them could I hope to detect and eliminate any undesirable elements before we sailed.

The officers allotted to me were endowed with a variety of talents. Some were regular career officers like my first lieutenant, Kühn, and my gunnery officer, Lieutenant Kasch; others, equally competent, came from the Merchant Navy, like the navigation officer, Captain Kamenz. There were also a number of officers from the Merchant Navy, all with mate's or master's certificates, who had been accorded the rank of sub-lieutenant (S) in the Navy; they would eventually take command of the prizes we hoped to capture. The (S) stood for "Special Service." I took a great deal of trouble to seek out the right men for these duties, for energy and courage of a high order would be required to sail a prize ship home through enemy-occupied waters with only a handful of men as crew, and perhaps the additional problem of rebellious prisoners.

Fortunately I was on the best of terms with Commander Winther of the Officers' Appointment Branch at Wilhelmshaven. He might beat his brow whenever he saw me approaching, yet he always tried to meet my requirements.

"I must have a new adjutant," I said to him one day. "The art historian you sent me is a charming fellow but quite helpless. You might appoint him to some port where there are lots of pictures. I need another type of man and I know just the fellow I want."

Winther gave an unenthusiastic groan, but I was determined to have my way. "I know you are short of officer recruits," I said. "I've got two reserve officer cadets whom nobody knows anything about. You can have them and my present adjutant in exchange for the new one."

And that was how Sub-Lieutenant Mohr came to join me in "Ship 16" from a depot ship where he had felt completely out of place. He was a reserve officer and held a degree in chemistry; a competent individual with very much a will of his own, he spoke several languages and looked older than his years.

My administrative officer, Commander Lorenzen, was also a reservist who in private life owned a textile factory. He might have been born for the job, with his wide experience, easy manners and ability to work with others. My principal medical officer, Dr. Reil, an officer on the active list, had already served under me in two training ships and I had frightful trouble before I managed to winkle him out of his position on the staff of the fleet medical officer but I had many good reasons for insisting on his appointment. Despite his irrepressible good humor and his inexhaustible fund of smoking room stories, Reil was not a man to be taken lightly. His lighthearted manner concealed a mature integrity which would make him invaluable as a mediator in the differences that were bound to arise among such a heterogeneous collection of officers. It remained to be seen how the assistant medical officer, Dr. Sprung, and the meteorological officer, Dr. Collmann, would fulfill their early promise; their professional ability was beyond question and the first impression they made was excellent.

The difficulties of converting the ship were wellnigh insuperable. If any proof were needed of how far the German Navy was from being ready to undertake a war against the greatest sea power in Europe, it was to be seen in the fitting out of a commerce raider. The Weser Company at Bremen gave me every possible support from the managing director downward, but the plain fact remained that, owing to lack of foresight on the part of the German Naval Staff, plans to convert the merchant ship into a raider simply did not exist. My officers and I, in consultation with the dockyard engineers, had to solve each problem as it arose; our decisions were committed to paper and thereafter served as building plans.

On two occasions I paid a visit to Commander Nerger, who had commanded the famous raider *Wolf* in the First World War, and who held the all-time raider record of 450 days at sea. From him I received many valuable hints, which compensated in some measure for the lack, or inaccessibility, of records of the Great War. For example, the flaps which hid the *Wolf*'s guns opened downward—an unpractical system because they not only made a lot of noise when operated but they failed to provide adequate protection from heavy seas. We made our flaps open upward by using counterweights.

In drawing up lists of stores and equipment, my first lieutenant, Kühn, had no precedent to follow; he had to rely on his own experience as to what we should take with us—but one thing he did not lack was experience. Having risen to the rank of lieutenant after thirty years of service beginning as boy in the Imperial Navy, he was well versed in the Navy's way of acquiring things, whether by orthodox means or otherwise. He knew when and where every ship had been paid off, whether she still contained anything of use to a raider, and how best it could be formally requisitioned or informally "nobbled." As a result, something useful was provided for our ship even by those naval storesheds which everyone else believed to contain nothing but rats and rubbish. For all that, Kühn's was no mean problem, for he knew as well as I did that any item overlooked now could never be made good once we had sailed.

In planning the accommodation I decided that each man should live close to his action station and that as many as possible should have their own bunks. Each officer had his own cabin; the CPOs were in single or double cabins; POs in four- or eight-berthed quarters; ratings in messes of from eighteen to fifty. The torpedo men slept near their tubes, the gunners near their guns and so on. The dockyard people were able to provide bunks for all except 50 men, who slept in hammocks. The additional timber required for the bunks would certainly add to the risk of fire during an engagement, but I held that the welfare of the crew was more important.

Besides dealing with all the problems of planning and supplies, I had to spend a lot of time traveling. I visited the Blohm & Voss yards at Hamburg to exchange ideas with the other raider captains and then went to Berlin for briefing by the Naval Staff and the Supreme Command of the Armed Forces. Meanwhile my crew was being trained at Bremenhaven. There were very few left from the original muster. The Drafting Office seemed to have been under the impression that they could unload on me all their riff-raff—men under punishment, confirmed idlers, anyone who had proved to be unemployable elsewhere. I had looked at these men with a very critical eye from the very beginning, and on my first muster on the barrack square I went carefully into the history of each man. As their commanding officer I was going to spend a year with these men—perhaps longer; now was the time to weed out the undesirables.

Out of the 214 men I dismissed 104 and next day I told the drafting commander that I should be unable to employ nearly 50 per cent of the men he had assigned to me. What I wanted, I told him, was a handpicked ship's company of good sound men; the high standard of the crew would have to compensate for the weakness of my ship's fighting powers. In particular there were twelve men from the *Schlageter* whom I wanted. The officer looked horrified at the mention of the *Schlageter*. "She's a Baltic-based ship!" he cried. "You know as well as I do that it's easier to pass a camel through the eye of a needle than to transfer a man from the Baltic depot to the North Sea!" However I got my way, and a fortnight later 104 men with first-class records joined "Ship 16," headed by the twelve men with Baltic depot numbers from my old command.

"Ship 16" had been built by the Bremen Hansa Line as the 7,860-ton freighter *Goldenfels*. She was 500 feet long, 60 feet wide, with a draught of 25 feet and a top speed of 17½ knots. It took the dockyard fourteen long weeks to convert her into an armed merchant cruiser; at times it seemed as though the ship would have to be so completely rebuilt that she would never be ready. But at last the day of her completion came in sight; her armament—six 6 inch guns, a 3 inch warning gun, two twin 3.7 cm AA guns and four 2 cm automatics—was completely invisible beneath the camouflage. On either side below the waterline amidships was a torpedo tube, while the mine compartment had stowage for 92 magnetic mines. No. 2 hold had been made into a hanger for a reconnaissance seaplane. We had been assigned one *He 114* fully assembled and a reserve machine in crates. I asked for a second spare plane but my request was turned down on the grounds that they were in short supply. My request, as it turned out, was fully justified.

He 114

On December 19, 1939, my ship was formally commissioned under the name of *Atlantis*. Eighty per cent of my crew were already on board and two days later we steamed down the Weser on acceptance trials. We then anchored off the Elbe where for the first time the camouflage party tried out their various gadgets.

It was astonishing what changes in the ship's appearance they were able to effect. A dummy funnel could be set up or stowed away at will, the real funnel could be lengthened or shortened; the masts were telescopic like the legs of a camera tripod; there were dummy guns made of wood, false platforms, huge crates representing deck cargo, and a whole heap of other devices. As the ship threaded her way through the ice floes at the mouth of the Elbe on her way to the Kiel Canal, I felt confident that nobody would have recognized the former *Goldenfels* in her twin-funneled garb of a large minesweeper.

Secrecy was all-important at this juncture. When the commander-in-chief of the Navy inspected us on January 31, accompanied by only a few of his personal staff, I arranged for him to slip on board unobtrusively and to leave again with as little outward fuss. Similarly, when lighters came alongside with mines or ammunition, we delayed unloading them until the tug which had brought them had been sent away.

At length came the month of March, with Easter approaching, and I was able to report to the Naval Staff that *Atlantis* was "in commission and ready for sea." Before going to Berlin to receive my final instructions I ordered all arrangements for Easter leave to go forward in the normal way; at the same time I asked for gunnery targets and everything needed for final firing practice off Pillau immediately after Easter. We did this to mislead possible foreign agents.

As soon as I had returned from Berlin I took the ship to sea. Half an hour before casting off I dismissed a man found guilty of disobedience and landed him, bag and baggage, on the jetty; he was replaced by another from a nearby barracks. We did not go to Pillau as announced but into the Holtenau Lock, where we took station astern of the old target ship *Hessen,* which was acting as icebreaker. We steamed through the Kiel Canal in company with "Ship 36" (*Orion*) and "Ship 21" (*Widder*), both raiders and commanded respectively by Captains Weyher and von Ruckteschell. All three ships carried minesweeper's distinguishing marks as additional camouflage. *Atlantis* and *Orion* carried out the rest of their firing program together and we then parted company.

Wearing Norwegian colors, *Atlantis* steamed into the Süderpiep, a small inlet on the west coast of Schleswig-Holstein, north of the Elbe. Here we lay at anchor until we received orders to sail.

Our destination: the Atlantic Ocean—and beyond.

2

NORTH ABOUT

After the long months of planning and fitting-out, our great voyage had begun. We steamed northward with an escort of two torpedo boats and some fighter aircraft, which remained with us until nightfall; but when the new day dawned over the gray North Sea our only companion was a U-boat steering a parallel course several miles off.

As night closed in, we removed the Norwegian disguise. The ship no longer displayed two funnels as she had in Kiel; now she was a Russian ship—to be exact, the Soviet auxiliary warship *Kim*. Cloaked in our new identity we steamed at high speed toward the first of the danger spots on our route; for according to air reconnaissance reports, the narrows between Western Norway and the Shetlands were closely guarded by British cruisers.

Ever since we had hove our anchor out of the mud of the Süderpiep, a fresh wind had blown from the southwest. The skies were clouded over and the sea was rising; the air was gray and heavy—scarce five miles visibility—with the temperature hovering just above zero. Visibility decreased still further at nightfall, when a curtain of clouds descended, masking the pale moon—just what we needed for making a dash through the narrows. The freshening breeze brought rain pelting down on the decks and superstructure.

A new dawn brought more wind, clouds and rain. We sighted nothing until evening, when three fishing boats appeared near the Klondyke Bank; but we held steadily to our northerly course. My radio operator reported that the ether was full of English five-letter code groups. Had we been spotted? As the day ended the wind freshened again, backing quickly from south to northeast and eventually blowing straight from the north at force 7 to 8, with rapidly rising seas. The U-boat signaled that she could no longer maintain her speed in such weather and we held a brief council of war. To reduce speed now would mean passing at an unfavorable time through the closely guarded narrows between Scotland and Bergen; in any case the raging sea had diminished the already doubtful value of the U-boat as escort. Finally I decided to proceed at top speed alone and to rendezvous later with the U-boat east of the Denmark Strait.

At first light the mastheads and funnels of two ships appeared beyond the mountainous seas. One of them carried no lights, the other displayed steaming and navigation lights and at short intervals showed a red masthead light; both ships were laboring heavily in the storm. From time to time they disappeared from view and during one of these intervals I seized the opportunity of altering course away from them. We steamed away at our best speed of 17½ knots. Under the thousands of horsepower driving her against the gale *Atlantis* shook from stem to stern as her bows lifted to one wave and her stern plunged into the trough of another. No captain makes such demands upon his ship without good cause; the moment the strange ships had vanished beneath the horizon, I reduced revolutions and the shaking and shuddering beneath our feet died away.

By 11:00 A.M. when the ship again turned northeast, the equinoctial gale had reached its height. As the clouds sped away the sun illumined a vast, heaving sparkling waste, flecked with foam and spindrift, its colors changing from dull gray to deepest blue and bottle-green. Now at its climax, the gale thundered over the ship with a deafening roar, lashing our faces and forcing us to screw up our eyes into narrow slits. By noon we had made good 624 miles since leaving harbor; we were now in the danger zone, crossing the Scotland-Norway shipping route, alert for any and every danger.

The first ship to be sighted was a Wilhelmsen Company freighter, later identified from radio messages as the *Taronga;* then came a pair of suspiciously lofty masts on an unusual course—almost certainly an armed merchant cruiser. Was this to be the end already? We held our breath as we kept our binoculars glued on her, until she turned sharply away and moved off at full speed. In the afternoon a German recce plane appeared—a *Dornier 26*—but until it had been identified

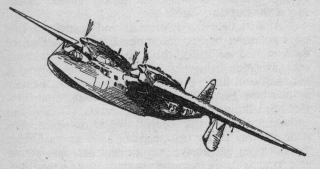

Dornier 26

as friendly, each second seemed a lifetime.

At last the violence of the storm was spent. The intervals between the squalls lengthened until the wind dropped to a light NNW breeze and the sea grew calmer, leaving only a northeasterly swell. As darkness fell the skies became streaked and shot through with brilliant, fan-shaped rays of colored light which flashed and gleamed the whole night through, while *Atlantis* ploughed steadily through the heavy swell, mile after mile through the Shetland Narrows, still steering a deception course for Murmansk but ultimately bound for the open spaces of the North Atlantic.

At 9 A.M. on the third day out we crossed the Arctic Circle, still on our simulated course for Murmansk. We did not swing around to the west until the evening; by that time we were so far north that our new course would arouse no curiosity. It followed the route from Murmansk to Iceland and would soon bring us to position "Nixe," where I hoped to meet the U-boat again. From there we could either break out to the north of Iceland or, if the ice conditions should make that impossible, we could take the more dangerous route to the south.

Our new course brought the ship once more into the teeth of wind and sea. The darkness became less intense as the clear sky glowed in the ever-changing Northern Lights, while greenish St. Elmo's fire danced from one point of the ship to another. Without a name, flying a foreign flag and showing false distinguishing marks, we went ploughing through the vast wastes of the Arctic Sea, our intentions secret, our true nature hidden, our cargo concealed, the crew disguised as Russians even to the cut of their hair.

The weather was improving visibly and the wind died away during the night; in the morning all was calm and the skies were frosty but crystal clear. Toward evening the U-boat appeared at point "Nixe" as arranged, showing up on the water as a thin straight line, her conning tower prominent amidships. She had been waiting there since the forenoon and had almost given up hope of meeting us; now she approached, grappled hold of a hose pipe and drew twenty-five tons of fuel and half a ton of lubricant from our reserves. I took this opportunity of telling the U-boat commander of my plans. No information was available as to ice conditions in the Denmark Strait, so I intended to find out for myself. The only current report mentioned much heavy drift ice north of Iceland but did not indicate whether the Strait was navigable. It seemed more likely than ever that I would have to take the southern route. While we were discussing our next meeting place a radio message came in: Meteorological report from 66°42′N, 24°40′W, light NE wind, visibility good. Limit of pack ice approximately from 66°48′N, 25°20′W to 67°12′N, 24°10′W to 67°30·N., 23° 10′W," and then a laconic final sentence, "Ice conditions permit passage north of Iceland by night."

The situation was now clear; we would attempt to break through by the northern route without further reconnaissance. I ordered the U-boat commander to remain close at hand, if possible within sight of the ship; should any strange ship be sighted at long range, he was to remain surfaced in company. I told him I would keep as close as I could to the pack ice barrier, making the most of the prevailing fog condititions. Weather reports showed that a strong NE wind—favorable to us—was blowing in those waters, whereas on the southern route it was coming from the opposite quarter. When the U-boat had completed refueling we resumed our westward journey at reduced speed, in order not to reach the Denmark Strait before evening.

During the afternoon the clouds dispersed, leaving a pale blue sky, clear and cold. As the wind rose the thermometer quickly dropped below freezing point; the sun's rays were pale and feeble. In the first dog watch we sighted the first ice floes—small round slabs riding the waves close together and keeping the sea flat. We were taking the temperature of the water at regular intervals; in two hours it dropped from 33° to 27°. Soon after midnight we encountered fields of ice floes which looked like plate-sized jellyfish, and I thought it advisable to head more to the south to avoid meeting larger floes in the dark. At dawn the wind was blowing with gale force from the northeast and steep heavy seas were racing after the ship. The water was at freezing point and the air was 19° below zero; the U-boat signaled that she would not be able to crash dive because of icing-up. This was hardly surprising as her low hull and tiny conning tower were continually being swept by heavy seas.

I was now waiting impatiently for an Icelandic weather report due to be relayed from Germany. When it came at last, after three hours, I read: "The leading edge of a depression south of Iceland extends to the north coast of the island with winds up to force 8 and snowdrifts." This decided me to break through by the Denmark Strait. I altered course more to the north to locate the ice barrier and to take advantage of the foggy conditions described in the sailing directions. The wind had increased to a full gale and the U-boat was struggling to keep station, though she was more often under the water than on the surface. I asked her commander two questions by signal:

"1. *What chances have you got of delivering an attack in an emergency?*
2. *Are you prepared to accompany me as far as the ice barrier?*"

In the intervals between the waves that swept the conning tower came his answer:

"1. *I will do my best. 2. Yes.*"

We continued in company toward the ice line, which we sighted at 3 P.M. in position 67°24′N, 24°W; the strong NE wind had packed the ice into a clearly defined edge. We proceeded parallel to the ice line in heavy, breaking seas. The vast windswept Arctic Sea lay empty; the ships of the British northern patrol which normally rolled their guts out in these icy waters had run for shelter to the fjords on the north coast of Iceland. Fog lay thick over the ice, but over the water visibility extended for a good five miles; the icefield itself consisted of small floes of drift ice with large blocks of hard blue-ice, behind which lay the icebergs. The edge of the icefield ran in a SW direction, with occasional indentations.

Shortly before dusk the U-boat signaled, *"No longer fit for action. Must heave-to as am in danger of flooding through conning-tower hatch."* I decided to stand by while the U-boat hauled up into the sea and then go on without her. The huge, bitterly cold seas which swept the length of the tiny vessel had covered the whole of her upper works with ice—superstructure, valve heads, coamings and hatches. While she was turning it seemed at times that the gigantic seas, rolling her more than 45 degrees from the vertical, would simply capsize her and bury her for ever, but gradually she got her head into the sea and lay there snugly.

As we turned back on our westerly course and increased speed, I signaled, *"Proceed independently.*

Many thanks for your escort. Best wishes to all at home." Through the failing daylight the U-boat's signal lamp blinked the parting words, *"Best of luck and a safe return.*" Within minutes the U-boat was out of our sight, while we continued steadily along the edge of the icefields in a howling northeaster. With the thermometer standing at 17 degrees below, every piece of steel on the upper deck seemed to glitter with the cold and the air cut like a knife into every inch of unprotected skin.

Next morning the edge of the ice barrier curved around to the west. The fury of the northeast wind was tearing great chunks of blue-ice and icebergs from the edge of the pack ice and driving them out into the Atlantic. For hours we had to con the ship with the utmost care to avoid them. When at length we entered the Gulf Stream at midnight it was like coming out of a cold winter's night into a warm room; in no time at all the temperature of the water rose from below freezing point to 42 degrees.

By dawn we had successfully negotiated the second danger spot on our route. As we steamed out of the Denmark Strait into the Atlantic the northerly wind dropped, leaving a cloudy sky and a slight haze along the edge of the Gulf Stream. The vital fact remained that we had not been sighted by any stranger. At noon, still heading southwest along the coast of Greenland, we intercepted a signal from the U-boat. It was addressed to the Naval Staff at the German Admiralty and read:

> *"Parted company with* Atlantis *in grid-square 2957 AD. Compelled to heave-to in north-easterly gale."*

In this way the commander-in-chief of the Navy learned that *Atlantis*—the first German armed merchant cruiser to sail in the Second World War—had made a successful breakthrough into the Atlantic Ocean. By 8 A.M. next morning we were abreast of Cape Farewell, the southernmost point of Greenland, and heading south into warmer and friendlier waters.

3

A NEW DISGUISE

Steaming for economy's sake at ten knots on one. engine, we headed into stormy winds and through snow squalls and fog, occasionally altering course to avoid icebergs and fields of pack ice. We were of course keeping strict wireless silence. Days went by with nothing seen or heard; the pleasant monotony of shipboard routine gave everyone a chance to settle down.

As we moved southward our radio operators picked up a stream of messages from passing ships— a Belgian tanker making for home, the Finnish *Fidra,* the Norwegian *Randersfjord,* then a British warship, apparently quite close, and an American fruit ship. One evening we sighted lights to port and turned due south at slow speed until they were lost to view; an encounter was the last thing we wanted at the moment, although chance meetings were becoming increasingly frequent. Every time a ship was sighted I altered course to avoid her, increasing to full speed again as soon as she was out of sight, for I wanted to get clear of this three hundred mile wide main trans-Atlantic shipping route in the shortest time.

As we steamed on, the fur-lined jackets and woolen clothing of the Arctic disappeared and in their place the crew wore "home rig," while the first white tunics appeared on the bridge. Soon I had to order the topmasts to be shortened by one step and the crow's nests to be removed; in these waters they were too conspicuous. The ether was now full of radio traffic; in a single day, April 11, our W/T office got D/F bearings of no less than eight transmissions from different ships in the vicinity, including Americans, Canadians, Italians and Belgians. At each dusk and dawn we steered a deception course toward Panama to allay the suspicions of any ship that might happen upon us in the failing light; we were keeping well to the west of the Azores, as it was better to take the long way around than to be sighted prematurely. On April 15 we reached the zone of the trades, which blew steadily as in the book, and the clouds drifted away, leaving the sun to blaze down from a clear sky.

Two days later came a signal from the Naval Staff: *"1814/57—Atlantis should expedite passage to South Atlantic and appear on Capetown-Freetown route as soon as possible in order to divert the enemy's attention from nearer home."* After reading this order I tried to recall everything that I had learned in the last few days from the Naval Staff's signals and from various broadcasts. It was little enough, yet sufficient to give an approximate picture of the situation in the North Sea, where there was a heavy concentration of enemy forces off the Norwegian coast, after a lightning thrust by the German armed forces had forestalled the Anglo-French invasion of Norway by a matter of hours. The Naval Staff rightly hoped that the appearance of the first raiders—*Atlantis* and *Orion*—would commit enemy forces to the North and South Atlantic just at the moment when all efforts should be concentrated on attacking the German invasion forces in Norway. If the raiders' sudden appearance and early successes managed to draw off some cruisers and possibly air craft carriers, this would provide a substantial relief to the still precarious German positions in Norway.

I decided to make for the Capetown-Freetown route, work my way into it and then run southward along it in wide sweeps. We would reach the route at about 12°S, 2°W—halfway between Ascension Island and St. Helena.

We were now in the midst of the trades. The PMO had given us our first typhus inoculation and all winter clothing had long since been stowed away.

"Tropical rig" was the order of the day and the ship-wrights had built a swimming pool on deck out of planks and sail cloth which was very popular. I took advantage of the calm sea to launch a cutter for a close inspection of the camouflage, particularly of the modified version of No. 5 gun. Disguised as "deck cargo" under a large crate covered with tarpaulins, the gun was even less noticeable than before. Thanks to incessant practice we could now throw off our disguise and be ready for action within two seconds.

We entered the doldrums. The northeast trade winds gradually died away and the massed clouds lost the shimmering gleam characteristic of the trades; rain fell at night and lightning flickered below the dark horizon. On the afternoon of April 22 *Atlantis* crossed the line but without ceremony as yet, for we were now at the narrowest point of the South Atlantic between Freetown in West Africa and Bahia on the coast of South America—and it would never do to let Neptune be confounded by Mars. Since the previous day our Naval Staff had begun to send out regular intelligence reports to us and *Orion* of the enemy's warship dispositions, their probable future movements and those of merchant shipping. It was thus possible to form a good picture of the situation; the North Sea was evidently attracting powerful forces, while a squadron was being assembled at Gibraltar at the expense of the Atlantic forces. British documents captured in Norway had revealed much of the organization and routes of enemy convoys—details that were of immeasurable value to a raider captain. I decided to continue south for three days before celebrating crossing the line, for until we had reached latitude 8°S there could be no relaxation; at the moment we had other things to think about.

Early one morning a ship with brightly burning lights passed ahead of us, her neutrality markings fore and aft showing clearly in the glare of her own arc lamps. We steered to give her a wide berth until intercepted signals revealed her as the Italian *Oceania* of 19,507 tons, a twenty-knot liner on passage from Genoa to Buenos Aires. Shortly afterward another ship loomed up and immediately extinguished her steaming lights, but we carried on as though nothing had happened and she soon disappeared.

In the forenoon we stopped engines; we were alone in the vast ocean, with the burning sun reflected in a million sparkles on the long, lazy swell. The first lieutenant put the men on to stripping off the ship's storm-damaged paint. The old paint, put on in wintry cold and dried off in unfavorable conditions, had flaked off in great patches during the northern gales, making the ship look like a salamander. The overside party were suspended on small stages; half-naked and flecked with paint, they cracked jokes despite the heat, while some of the off-duty watch trailed shark lines over the side—the sport of seafaring men down the ages—with big hooks baited with meat or bacon. The hungry robbers were soon on the spot; they had been following the ship for days—triangular fins in the wake, an occasional glimpse of a white belly and a lightning dash each time a galleyhand tipped a bucket of gash over the side. Now they met the same end as scores of their ancestors down the centuries—torn from their natural element, a knife driven into their throat and the shipwright's axe to finish them off.

On Wednesday, April 24, the ceremony of crossing the line took place at long last. A traditionally garbed Triton came aboard the evening before with a crowd of satellites to announce the arrival of His Splendid Majesty Neptune, "Lord of all Seas, Lakes, Ponds, Puddles, Rivers, Streams and Morasses, who will be accompanied by his All-Charming and All-Gracious Spouse, Thetis." Now came the High Lord with his High Lady and their retinue—Actuarius, the Barber, the Astronomer, the Police and scores of niggers, to celebrate the baptism of some 250 novices by subjecting them to hefty duckings, thereby cleansing them of the dust of the northern hemisphere. In the afternoon there was "make and mend clothes," coffee, cakes and an extra ration of beer.

While the festivities were continuing below decks, I divested myself of the "high orders" I had received and settled down to contemplate the immediate future.

In a few days we should reach the Capetown-Freetown route and start looking for some ships. But first *Atlantis* would have to change her disguise, for in these waters a Russian auxiliary cruiser would be an anachronism. Whereas in more appropriate disguise the enemy would have no reason to suspect us, even if we were to attack and seize a couple of ships—provided that our victims were prevented from sending out a distress signal, the regulation "QQQ" for "have sighted a suspicious vessel" or "RRR" for "raider." Everything depended upon allaying the suspicions of any passing neutrals—the success not only of this operation but also of our plans to lay mines off Cape Agulhas on the coast of South Africa.

I had originally intended to disguise the ship as a Scandinavian, but the Norwegian campaign precluded that, so we searched through Lloyd's Register of Shipping for all motorships built since 1930 with a cruiser stern and displacing between 5,000 and 10,000 tons, giving preference to those which in some particular already resembled *Atlantis*. Of all the world's merchant navies the choice was finally found to lie between twenty-six ships—five Americans, two Italians, two French, one Belgian, two Dutch, four Greek and eight Japanese. The Americans had to be excluded as their call signals were unknown; the French, Belgian and Dutch ships seemed unsuitable, as British agents would probably be keeping the enemy informed of their movements; the Greeks were also ruled out because their characteristic color scheme would be too conspicuous in the South Atlantic. That left only the Japanese cargo-carrying companies, about whose color schemes very little information was available; but we did at least know that the Kokussai Company's ships did not carry white stripes on their sides like some others and so our choice fell upon that company's *Kasil Maru* of 8,408 tons, registered in Tokyo, built in 1936, call sign JHOJ. *Atlantis*'s hull was duly painted black, her masts yellow, her ventilators yellow outside and red inside, her funnel black with a red boot-top and a white "K." The upper works presented no difficulty but when the ship was stopped for repainting the water-

line, it was found that the old paint, strongly impreg-
nated with salt, had never really dried on; hence the
new coat, painted over a damp surface, soon washed
off. This problem of the waterline paint was never sur-
mounted throughout the cruise. Nevertheless having inspected the changes from a cutter, I felt satisfied with
the result.

After Sunday divisions and divine service on April
28, 1940, I addressed my ship's company. I remember
saying to them, "In a few days from now we shall no
longer take avoiding action whenever we meet a ship
—we shall close in to attack. Then you will be able to
to judge for yourselves the value of all the trouble we
have taken." I reminded them that our task was not to
sink every ship we sighted, but to spread alarm and
despondency among the enemy, to force him to sail
his ships in escorted convoys and to upset the economy
of his dominions and colonies. "We must use every
trick and ruse we can think of," I said. "If anyone has
a suggestion to make, he should not keep it to himself; by passing it on to me he will be helping us all toward a common victory." The length of time we could
continue to operate in any one area would depend
entirely, I added, upon the skill and perfection of our
disguise. As soon as we were located we would have
to disappear into some unfrequented area beyond the
reach of enemy patrols. We might have to spend
long periods inactive, for as long as the enemy was
left in doubt as to our whereabouts he would be forced
to waste valuable time and energy in fruitless search.

"There is one further point," I concluded. "We
shall on no account become involved in action with
enemy warships or auxiliary cruisers. But if this proves
unavoidable we shall make use of our disguise until
the last possible moment and then try to destroy the
enemy by a surprise attack. Nor shall we attack convoys or passenger ships, as they will generally be superior to us in speed and armament; and even if we
succeeded in destroying them, their crews and passengers would prove an embarrassment to us."

By the next day our Japanese disguise was complete. Bespectacled dark-haired ratings, wearing white

head scarves and shirts outside their trousers, could be seen moving about the decks. A "woman" was pushing a pram; on the boat deck six "Japanese passengers" lay in deck chairs. All was ready for our first victim. But in the days that followed we sighted nothing; a gale blew up from ESE and the steep seas sent spray flying over the bridge as our bows dipped slowly into the blue waves while the ship shuddered from stem to stern. This was hardly the weather for stopping and searching ships—and it was growing worse.

On the evening of May 1 the German and Italian radio stations broadcast that Britain had decided to divert her Mediterranean shipping. How reliable was this news? Did it emanate from the British Foreign Office? Could "diversion of shipping" mean anything less than abandoning the Mediterranean and sending ships around the Cape of Good Hope? If that were the case, it would have been wiser to lay mines off Cape Agulhas first, as I had originally intended before the Naval Staff ordered me to attack the Capetown-Freetown route. But it was too late to change our plans now—and anyway, orders are orders.

4

THE BAPTISM OF FIRE

For three days we searched along the Capetown-Freetown route. Then on Thursday May 2, 1940, our masthead lookout sighted a smoke cloud on the port bow. I immediately turned 40 degrees to port to close the stranger: the "Japanese" took their places on deck and everyone else disappeared from view. The W/T office reported that a Belgian ship, the *Thysville*, was busily transmitting in the neighborhood. Just as the masthead lookout was calling down his telephone, "Enemy's funnel in sight," the *Thysville* broke off her transmission in the middle of a sentence.

A few minutes later the strange ship appeared over the horizon. Her gray hull and black funnel seemed to confirm that she really was the *Thysville* belonging to the Lloyd Royal Cie. Maritime Belge, and as she swept past us nine miles off we could see that she was a fairly large passenger ship. We gradually altered course away—attacking passenger ships was a thankless task; her presence at any rate confirmed that we were in the right shipping lane. But as she held on her course to pass us we realized that she could not be the *Thysville*. The ship was armed with a gun of about 4.5 inch caliber on a platform aft and light AA guns on her superstructure. Could she be an auxiliary cruiser? She was now within seven miles of us and judging by the number of boats—three on either side of the boat deck and one aft—and by the appearance of the boat deck itself, she was carrying a lot of passengers. As she was certain to send out an SOS signal if approached, I decided not to interfere with her. She went on her way at high speed, steering north-northwest, without hoisting a flag or manning her guns. With her straight stem and cruiser stern she looked like one of the Ellerman liners such as the *City of Exeter* or *City of Venice* of about 8,000 tons, carrying one hundred and seventy to two hundred passengers.

The next afternoon another ship appeared. My coxswain first sighted the thin smoke cloud rising like a downy feather over the horizon. A fresh trade wind was blowing and the sea was running fairly high; visibility varied, now limited by haze, now extending to a clear horizon. As soon as I had picked up the streamer of smoke in my glasses I sounded the alarm and ordered full speed on both engines. There was a clatter and stamping of hurrying feet as the crew raced to action stations, then a tense silence broken only by the voice of the gunnery officer as he issued corrections from the rangefinder.

The enemy's funnel appeared at 2:07 P.M. and I turned sharply to port; the ship was steering a course which would bring her across our bows from starboard to port. The range was about 17,000 yards; it was still too early to identify the enemy properly. But as her hull came into view we could see that she had a red band on her funnel, that she carried no flag, but that there was a gun aft. Her wireless cabin was directly abaft her funnel. Within half an hour the range had dropped to 10,400 yards and so far neither of us had appeared to take any notice of the other. Our target had certainly not realized that we had altered our speed three times in eleven minutes to keep the bearing constant, for she was holding steadily to her course.

Kasch called out the range at regular intervals from his rangefinder, which was disguised as a water-tank. Ten minutes crawled by, then we ran up the signal to heave-to on our yard arm and the German ensign was broken at the gaff. For the first time I gave in earnest the order that we had so often rehearsed: "Uncover the guns!"

The 3.7 cm could not yet be brought to bear so we sent a warning shot from the 7.5 cm. gun deliberately wide. The enemy steamed calmly on, hoisting the international flag signal for "Half," which did not make any sense to us. I ordered the starboard 6 inch guns to fire, still aiming wide; their shells churned up two white pillars of water ahead of the ship. The enemy merely hoisted the answering pennant, and maintained her course and speed so that the range began to drop quickly. We had to alter course abruptly in order to continue the action. The enemy blew off steam and appeared to stop, then turned sharply to starboard and steamed off at full speed.

All this happened in some thirty seconds. We came back quickly on to our old course to keep the sun behind us and at 3:03 P.M. I gave the starboard 6 inch guns permission to fire directly at the target. The first salvo hit aft and when the ship did not stop, a second salvo landed beneath her bridge on the port side. An evil-smelling cloud of yellow cordite billowed over *Atlantis,* while grayish clouds poured from the shell holes in the enemy. I ceased fire to observe the effect of our shooting; I did not want to endanger more human

lives than was necessary nor to waste valuable ammunition. But just as I did so, my W/T office reported that
the enemy was using her wireless. Our guns re-opened
fire. The next four salvoes missed owing to a defect on
the range-correction gear—the equipment had worked
perfectly for two months but it chose this moment to
break down! But more by luck than good judgment
one of our salvoes tore away the British ship's aerial
after she had transmitted her distress signal "QQQ"
eight times; and through our glasses we could see the
wires trailing over her radio cabin. Our fourth salvo
straddled her, one shell hitting amidships.

I ordered the flaps to be opened of the port side 6
inch guns; in the event of a prolonged engagement we
might have to open fire to port. But as we turned to
starboard the enemy turned to port, stopped and blew
off steam; her stern was in flames and her crew were
tumbling into the boats. We promptly ceased fire. A
few minutes later our motor launch was in the water
and heading across to the enemy. It made fast alongside and the boarding party dashed up the gangway to
be met by the captain and first officer; they were the
only members of the crew who had remained on
board, the others were in the boats lying alongside or
pulling over toward *Atlantis*.

The English master greeted Mohr with icy politeness and answered his questions slowly and carefully.
His ship was the *Scientist* of 6,200 tons, owned by
Harrison & Co., of Liverpool, bound from Durban to
Liverpool with a cargo of copper bars, chrome ore,
asbestos fiber, maize, hides and zinc concentrate. While
he was being questioned, the boarding party spread out
through the ship and made a quick examination of her.
No. 5 hatch cover was off and the hold was in flames,
but whether from our shell fire or deliberate action
could not be ascertained. There could be no question of
putting the fire out—the hold was just one glowing
mass.

The after gun, which stood untouched, was a 5
inch weapon made in 1918, with a sliding breech-
block and no night-sight illumination. A shell had
exploded close by it and our men looked with profes-

sional pride at the jagged hole torn by their 6 inch shell. Abaft the bridge, where the radio cabin had stood, they found only a heap of débris and tumbled sandbags which had completely buried the cabin. Mohr searched in vain for secret papers; the drawers in the master's cabin were empty and the master readily admitted that he had thrown their contents overboard. Nevertheless there was still some valuable booty to be had— books, charts, papers, the contents of the chart house wastepaper basket—everything went into the gaping maw of the boatswain's bag, to be evaluated later on board *Atlantis*. The officer in charge of the demolition party reported that the scuttling charges were in position. The boarding party went over the side and towed the life boats clear before the fuses were lit. However the *Scientist* did not sink until she had been hit by some more 6 inch salvoes and one torpedo.

There were nineteen white men, one white passenger and fifty-seven Lascars in the boats. Two men had been wounded. The radio operator had been hit in the head and arms by splinters which had to be removed under anesthetic; one Lascar who had been hit in the stomach died before we could operate on him.

In the growing dusk we steamed south at twelve knots, heading back along the course that our victim had been following and zigzagging slightly across it. There was little peace below decks that evening; everyone was highly excited over the day's events and the eleven members of the boarding party had to describe over and over again every detail of what they had seen in the enemy ship. Questions were fired at them from all directions. Was she well found? Had our shelling done much damage? Couldn't they have put the fire out? Had they got any loot? Hadn't it been an eerie sensation to go creeping into the bilges of a strange ship when, for all they knew, the time fuses of the scuttling charges might already be burning? Had anyone noticed how the crew was accommodated? Did white men and colored share the same quarters?

In the operating theater Dr. Sprung, assisted by Dr. Reil, removed the splinters from the radio operator's head and arms. The wounds looked ghastly—

wood splinters make worse holes than steel. With Mohr, Kamenz and the wireless officer, I examined the documents found on board. The interrogation of the prisoners had been interesting enough but these papers were full of information. First in importance to us was the revelation that all British merchant ships had black or gray hulls, while their upper works were painted brownish-yellow. Armed with this knowledge we would now be able to transform the raider into a British ship—a great advantage on a route such as this which was predominantly used by the British.

The second item of information was that British ships were completely blacked out at night, without even navigation lights. Thirdly it was clear that the British had never dreamed of the presence of German warships in these waters, so that between Durban and Sierra Leone there was no effective protection by the Royal Navy. The convoy system was only in operation from Freetown toward the United Kingdom; the *Scientist* was due out from there in convoy shortly after her arrival on May 10. On her last voyage she had not sighted a single ship until she met us.

Papers taken from the wireless cabin included the wireless watch rosters of other ships and the deciphering table; we learned that British ships maintained complete wireless silence at sea and did not use foreign call signs, only such secret call signs as were laid down in the "Instructions for Communications by Armed Merchant Ships in Wartime," dated November, 1938. This handbook was of the greatest value to us. Mohr had also found a handbook on firing practice and instructions on what to do if attacked while sailing independently or in convoy.

The white and colored prisoners were given separate accommodation. This was no easy matter as space on board was limited, but it was essential to maintain the principle of separating whites from blacks. The colored men had fairly spacious quarters but the whites were rather cramped until the mine compartment had been emptied. I arranged for the white prisoners to receive the same food as my ship's company, but an Indian cook was detailed off to prepare rice, sardines, oil and various Asiatic delicacies for the colored men. I am very fond of a good curry myself, and it was not long before I had got this Indian to teach my own cook how to prepare rice in the proper way. I like my rice dry, with every grain separate, but in spite of frequent remonstrances, up to now I had always been served with a wet, messy pulp. That was soon altered! The first time my ship's company tasted rice cooked in the Indian fashion they licked their lips and now, at their annual reunions fifteen years later, they still order "rice *à la Atlantis*" for their main dish.

In my written analysis of the action I observed that our procedure for going into action had worked perfectly and that the camouflage devices had functioned without a hitch. The British officer of the watch had said his suspicions had never been aroused; on the other hand the ship's master had said that, given sufficient warning, he would have realized that *Atlantis* was not Japanese at five or six miles. He would not say why. He had apparently mistaken the *Atlantis* for a German-built ship operating in South American service. I also recorded in my log that owing to a misunderstanding the boarding party had only taken 40 lbs. of explosive with them, which was why the *Scientist* took so long to sink; I made a note that in the future they must take 200 lbs. We had kept one of the *Scientist*'s boats, I added, and sunk the rest by gunfire after stripping them of everything useful.

We had had our baptism of fire. What next? Our mines were still on board. The *Scientist* was not due in Freetown until May 10 and the enemy's suspicions would not be aroused until one or two days after that date. Now was the time to lay the mines.

Keeping well clear of all approach positions and coastal routes, we rounded the Cape and shaped course well to the southeast before closing Cape Agulhas. No one would suspect a westbound ship coming from Malaya or Australia of being a minelayer.

5

MINELAYING MISSION

The weather remained fine, with a light wind driving long low waves toward the ship; the sun was hot and the clouds white and fleecy. Our newly recruited Indians worked contentedly on deck and in the rigging, laughing and chattering as they chipped rust. Our gunners carried out exercises on the practice loader against a stop watch, and the English prisoners played cards on deck. For days on end we steamed south without sighting a thing. I was steering a course well out of range of South African land-based air patrols and away from the established positions I had noted in the *Scientist*'s papers. Each day's run brought us some three hundred miles nearer our goal.

On the morning of May 10 we were just twenty-four hours away from Cape Agulhas, sufficiently far to the southeast to give the impression that we had come from Australia. On this same day the German Army was advancing from the Siegfried Line to attack France and the Low Countries. I adjusted speed to be sixty miles from the start of the "lay" at 5:00 P.M.; for the last four hours of the run-in I planned to steam at fifteen knots. Despite the unusually fine weather I had not changed my plans; each day that we postponed the operation would mean less favorable conditions of moon. The Whitsun weekend was almost upon us, when a holiday atmosphere would be prevailing on shore. The whole of South Africa was probably glued to its loudspeakers at this time, listening for news of the German advance; so that despite the good visibility;

conditions were particularly favorable for laying our mines.

At 8:30 P.M. we went to action stations. As it grew darker the sea became luminous and the ship seemed to be sailing through liquid metal, her wake and bow wave glittering with phosphorescence while all around us flickered a ghostly blue-white fire. Visibility was still extraordinarily good; when dusk came at 5:00 P.M. we had been able to see the Cape Agulhas light at fifty-five miles, although it is only supposed to have a range of twenty miles. By the time the moon had set, the Agulhas light had attained the hard brilliance of a searchlight, swiveling rhythmically around like the bars of a giant capstan. Beyond the Cape rose the dark and menacing outline of the South African mainland, with jagged mountaintops and broad foothills; here and there a light shone from a window, a car's headlamps raced through the night, and again and again the Agulhas light swept over the ship, lighting up her white superstructure so that we all ducked involuntarily.

The minelaying ports in the stern had been opened at 8:45 P.M. and the minelaying party was standing by, reinforced by forty men from the guns. When the mining officer reported that all was ready, I gave permission to commence the lay; thereafter mine after mine went overboard at regular intervals. The calm sea made it easy to bring the mines up to the ports and although these were only 5½ feet above the waterline, we only once took water on board. By the time the sky began to lighten the Agulhas Bank—an area stretching from five to twenty-six miles off the Cape—had been sown with ninety-two mines at depths between twenty-five and sixty fathoms, laid in rows carefully plotted to coincide with the estimated course of ships steaming around the point. We completed the lay without a single interruption or mishap. A few passing neutral ships had been located by D/F and one aircraft was sighted off the Cape as we steamed away, but it paid no attention to us. I ordered the quartermaster to steer east-southeast and increased speed to sixteen knots.

It was important that any ship running on to one of our mines should think it had been laid by a U-boat, not by a surface ship, so we decided to manufacture some evidence of this. A damaged lifebuoy was painted gray with a smudged-over "U 37" on it and then thrown overboard in the hope that the enemy would find it. Next day we shaped course in the direction of Australia; we would lose nothing by doing so and I wanted to avoid arousing suspicion just as we were entering our new operational area—the Indian Ocean.

It was Sunday morning and after divine service I spoke to the men about the tactical principles behind the minelaying operation. Then I announced that we would carry out a special "camouflage exercise," expressly designed to deceive our prisoners as to what had really happened. I had decided that we were going to "rendezvous with a U-boat."

As experienced seafarers, the prisoners naturally had a pretty fair idea of what we had been doing since their capture, but while the minelaying had not gone unnoticed among them, they did not know where the minefield lay. It would not be difficult for them to work this out; they had noted the length of each day's run, the alteration of the ship's clocks when we reached the longitude of 15°E and other departures from routine such as the alteration in mealtimes, the darkening of the ship before the run-in and the setting of special watches; and they had drawn their own conclusions. Conclusions that would not be quite accurate as regards position but which in all probability were near enough.

In their opinion, *Atlantis* had laid her mines off Durban—the English skipper made no bones about it —because they did not realize how far to the south and southeast we had really steered. As a result their calculations by dead reckoning put them much more to the east than was in fact the case; they would be all the more astonished when the raider "met a U-boat" in that position.

Early next morning the prisoners were politely shepherded to their quarters on some flimsy excuse and shortly afterward the ship stopped engines. I hailed the imaginary U-boat commander through a megaphone and there was a pause during which the latter appeared to answer. I hailed him again and finally a boat was launched amid the shouting of orders, the "talking" of blocks and the crash of dangling falls against the ship's side. There was another pause while one diesel was run in short spurts as though the ship were being maneuvered and then, after the gangway had been hoisted out very noisily level with the prisoners' quarters, a boatswain "piped the side" as the "U-boat commander" came on board. Next came the typical sounds of guests being entertained—laughter from the ward room, singing in the crew's quarters; finally the boatswain piped the "U-boat's liberty men" over the side, followed by their officers, and after another interval our siren sounded three long notes in farewell. The ceremony was over.

That evening Mohr reported to me that it had been a complete success. The prisoners had followed every move; they hinted discreetly that it had been quite unnecessary to hide anything from them by making them stay in their quarters, and showed visible pride in their powers of perception. Mohr naturally kept a straight face when denying that *Atlantis* had met any other ship, let alone a U-boat. At dusk we altered course again to 140° to make some southing during the dark hours, reverting to our Australia course at dawn. We were now out of range of pursuit from the air and the AA crews could fall out and get some well-earned rest.

On Whit-Monday we reached 30° east and set clocks one hour forward. The thermometer had dropped to 62 degrees and we began to wear warm clothing again. I gave a small and select party at which the master of the *Scientist* was present. With the whiskey flowing freely we got the information that the fast liner we had sighted on May 2 was in fact not the Belgian *Thysville* but, as we had surmised, the Ellerman liner *City of Exeter*. However, as the *City of Exeter* was the only ship which had seen *Atlantis* in her Japanese disguise, I decided not to alter it; as the *Kasii Maru* we could hardly be less conspicuous in our

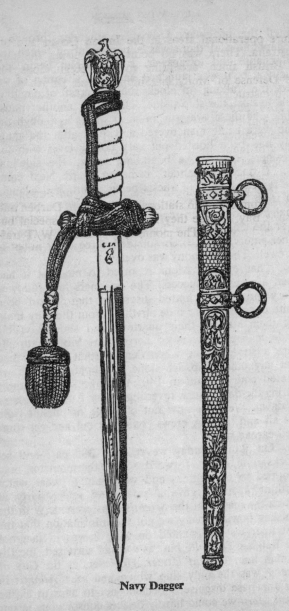

Navy Dagger

future operational areas in the Indian Ocean and off
Australia. There was no point in disguising the ship
as British since, according to the "Regulations for
the Defense of Merchant Shipping," all British ships
were instructed to avoid direct encounters with other
ships. I plotted a course which would bring us by
night into the southern latitudes—as far as 41° south
if the weather allowed. This would give us an opportunity of launching the seaplane on a trial flight, overhauling paintwork and allowing officers and men a
much needed period of rest.

We were keeping a regular watch on announce-
ments from the radio stations at Capetown, Durban and
Walvis Bay, in case they reported anything special but
we heard nothing. The monitoring of enemy W/T traffic was one of our most fruitful sources of information
and we kept permanent watch on all wavelengths.
Some of the messages were in code but there were just
as many *en clair,* particularly the weather reports,
which were of special interest to Dr. Collmann, who
used them to build up his slender stock of information
about weather conditions off the Cape.

I had decided not to make any further attacks
on enemy shipping for the time being but to "lie doggo";
this would give time for the minefield to take effect
and, in combination with the U-boat lifebuoy, would
give the enemy several headaches. I kept on course
80°—nearly due east—because I did not want to get
too far into the "Roaring Forties." During the forenoon of May 15 we picked up the usual broadcast
from Capetown: *"GBMS—to all British merchant
ships. Nothing to report."* But at 10 o'clock that evening the situation suddenly changed. The senior naval
officer, Simonstown, broadcast the following warning:
*"Important. To all British and Allied merchant ships.
In view of unconfirmed reports of an explosion south
of Agulhas all ships are warned to keep well clear of
the Agulhas Bank. T.O.O. 141013."* Our mines were
at work.

The signal did not give the name of this first victim but from intercepted messages she was probably
the Norwegian tanker *Jotnerfield* of 8,642 tons, which

had failed to answer signals for several days. It was reasonable to assume that our mines had been discovered, as lively enemy W/T traffic continued throughout the night, but it was three days before this was officially confirmed by a signal from the British naval commander-in-chief about the presence of minelayers off the South African coast. This signal was preceded by others from Simonstown warning all ships to keep outside the 100-fathom line because of both moored and drifting mines off Cape Agulhas, I was worried about the mention of drifting mines. I did not know then that by some error the mooring wires supplied to us in Germany were too weak and that, as a result, a number of mines had broken away in heavy seas. For days afterward the admiral at Simonstown was preoccupied with our legacy. *"Mines reported five miles south of Durban. All ships are warned to steer diversion courses to Durban."* This signal was sent out at regular intervals. At length we got a D/F bearing on the Norwegian *Bronnöy* of 4,791 tons, which was vainly trying at full power to communicate with Lourenço Marques and Madagascar. She was three hundred miles off the peacetime route from Australia to Durban—so that was where ships had been diverted!

We followed these events at long range, being all the more pleased that our labors had borne fruit because the sea around us was empty and the horizon remained unbroken. Meanwhile the news of the Agulhas minefield had reached Berlin, where the official propaganda machine made a very undesirable to-do about it all. The success of the operation was exaggerated and what particularly annoyed me was that the enemy were derided for not being able to catch one lone raider. That may have sounded all right from an armchair in Berlin but we on board the raider saw nothing welcome in the enemy being stimulated to greater activity against us. Enemy W/T traffic showed that the whole area was up in arms; anxiety reigned audibly as far away as India. It was not difficult to imagine how businessmen and shipowners were changing their plans, how insurance rates, freight rates and credits were rising and passengers were canceling their bookings. Since the *Wolf* had sailed from South African waters to lay mines off the shores of India in the Great War, her successor—or perhaps a U-boat—could equally well mine the entrances to Indian harbors twenty-five years later.

We would have to reckon with strong countermeasures being brought into operation against us.

PART TWO

THE INDIAN OCEAN

May–December 1940

6

UNDER DUTCH COLORS

On the evening of May 20 we intercepted a disturbing signal from Flag Officer, Colombo, warning all ships of the probable presence of "German raiders disguised as Japanese ships" in the Indian Ocean. The Admiral asked for sighting reports of all suspicious-looking vessels and gave notice that Aden, Port Sudan and the East African harbors would in future be closed at night; ships were ordered to show dimmed lights only at night and to black-out completely when west of 70° east. There could be no doubt that this description of our Japanese disguise was based on reports from the *City of Exeter,* whose suspicions had been aroused by the sight of a Japanese ship steering such an unusual course around the Cape.

I immediately altered course due east and then veered to south, in order to keep just clear of the Australia-Durban route; and I ordered the camouflage to be changed. Of the few remaining alternatives, my choice fell upon the Dutch m.v. *Abbekerk.* We began work the very next day. Squally weather was blowing up from the east with the seas steep and high, but I laid the ship beam on to the sea and listed her over by flooding her tanks, so that the neutrality markings on her sides could be completely erased.

The work sheet required to transform the *Kasii Maru* into the *Abbekerk* read as follows:

1. Paint out Japanese national markings with black.
2. Paint out ship's name at bow and stern.

3. Funnel: change red boot-topping with white "K" to black boot-topping with orange band.

4. Paint over national markings on upper bridge and control positions with brown.

5. Paint masts, topmasts and derricks in Dutch colors.

6. Paint ventilators and air shafts on upper deck, boat deck and poop deck, reddish-orange.

7. Change red paint on winch drums to white.

8. Gray-green winches to be painted light-green and black.

9. Black ventilators near funnel to be painted inside.

10. Paint shutter frames, smoke floats, bitts and goosenecks battleship-gray.

11. Change cipher books.

12. Stow Japanese ensign, bend on Dutch ensign and house flag.

Within twenty-four hours the change-over was complete and the Dutch motor ship *Abbekerk* was rolling in the heavy swell where the *Kasii Maru* had so lately been.

The ship of course had also changed her "owners." The *Abbekerk* was a 7,889-ton ship belonging to the Vereenigde Nederlandsche Scheep Vaarts My, NV. She had been built at Schichau in 1939. We had no actual photographs of her—only a photostat taken from a British book dated 1935, which gave her estimated silhouette. However, when the work was finished I felt that once again it would be difficult to distinguish the raider from the real *Abbekerk,* which was probably somewhere at sea at that very moment and almost certainly working for the British.

The weather at last improved enough to allow the seaplane pilot, Lieutenant Bulla, to make a couple of trial flights. Heedless of fuel consumption, he stayed up for two hours each time, covering wide stretches of the Australia route, but he saw nothing. He repeated his flight each day and although he did not sight anything, his crew and the crane party grew more experienced in handling the plane with each take-off and landing. Once they broke a float; once the plane was slung askew and crashed against the ship's side while being hoisted by the crane. The engine broke off and sank and the fuselage was damaged, but the air crew managed to patch the fragile machine up and make it airworthy again. Twenty-five years earlier the *Wolf* had also had a recce plane known as the "Wolfcub"; it would seem to have been more suited for the task than its successors, the first of which was written off exactly one week after its first take-off. I wrote in my log: "In future we will only launch the seaplane when it is absolutely vital to make an aerial reconnaissance. It would seem that the development of naval aircraft has not kept pace with other types of plane."

After days of fruitless search along the shipping routes between Australia and South Africa, I decided to sweep in shallow zigzags along the route from Australia to Mauritius, in the hope of finding a heavier concentration of traffic. I calculated that if ships were not using the recognized routes, they must be moving further afield.

Owing to his good knowledge of English, one of Mohr's many chores was to listen-in to neutral and enemy news bulletins. While listening one day to the American commentator in San Francisco he suddenly started and looked again at the notes he had been mechanically jotting down. "Dutch m.v. *Abbekerk* sunk in position . . ." For one shocking moment I thought that we would have to disguise our ship all over again, but then I remembered that a whole series of "kerk" ships were being built. I decided to leave *Atlantis* as she was for the time being.

It was the forenoon of June 10, 1940, and the news of the cessation of hostilities between Germany and Norway had just come through. A lookout reported mastheads on our starboard beam, so we started off in pursuit. It was our first chase in five long and uneventful weeks—not counting the night off Agulhas.

The foretop lookout reported that the ship had five polemasts and a short funnel set fairly well aft. Could she be a tanker? We turned at high speed to

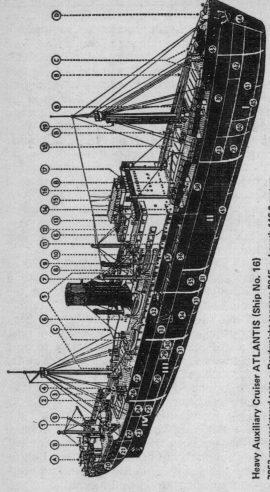

Heavy Auxiliary Cruiser ATLANTIS (Ship No. 16)

7862 gross registered tons · Deadweight tonnage 8945 · Length 146.2 meters
7600 horsepower engine · 2 MAN-motors · Speed 17 knots
Built 1937 by Vulcan Shipyard, Bremen; rebuilt 1939, in 99 days, by Weser
A.G., Bremen.

1. Reserve and isolation hospital
2. Laundry
3. Motor boat on Hold V
4. Pig pens
5. Motor lifeboats, one each starboard and port
6. Physician
7. Bakery
8. Life boats
9. Galley, library opposite on port side
10. Main hospital with operating room, pharmacy, etc.
11. Officers
12. Commander
13. Officers' mess and smoking room
14. First Officer
15. Fire control center
16. Officers' cabins
17. Bridge
18. Hold II containing flight-ready aircraft
19. Position of hoist for launching aircraft
20. Petty officers' washrooms and cabins
21. Mines, munitions (later, hold for colored prisoners)
22. Alternate hold for prisoners
23. Magazines
24. Ballast and chicken coop
25. Captured goods
26. Canteen
27. Crew's quarters
28. Provision hold and stern cooling system
29. Coal bunker
30. Stokehold
31. Double-bottom diesel fuel compartment
32. Large crew quarters
33. Middle cold-storage chamber
34. Main engine room
35. Forward electric generator
36. Large and small compartments for prisoners
37. Torpedo and crew quarters with torpedo tubes
38. Aircraft with spare parts
39. Forward crew quarters starboard and port
40. Sonar room
41. Sand ballast
42. Cabin for women and children
43. Carpenter's workshop
44. Collision bulkhead
45. Double-bottom compartments for oil, and fresh water storage

Armament

A Double 3.7-centimeter canons
B 15-centimeter canons
C 2-centimeter anti-aircraft under camouflage covering
D 7.5-centimeter signalling canon

I-V Cargo holds

intercept her; Kasch estimated the range at 32,000 yards. The alarm bells for action stations shrilled through the ship and the Indians working on deck were quickly herded below. Thirty minutes later we had almost halved the distance and could see every detail of the enemy. She carried a gun aft but it was still trained astern. My officers reckoned that she was one of the *Veltevreden* class or—when she was reported to have a blue funnel with a black top—to be a Blue Funnel liner; but we could not be sure as yet and the funnel looked rather too short. When the distance was down to 9,000 yards we began to turn five degrees at a time, reducing the range as unobtrusively as possible, but very soon the enemy ship altered away and appeared to increase speed; the two ships started to race each other but on courses that converged so slightly that the range closed very slowly.

We kept our diesels running at full speed for nearly three hours; my chief engineer and his men did magnificently, but it was soon obvious that if we were to overhaul the enemy, we would have to get the last ounce of power out of our engines. Before we could open fire the range had to be low enough to ensure the destruction of the enemy's wireless with our first salvo. At 10:55 we again altered five degrees toward our victim; the range was now 8,000 yards. Nine minutes later our guns were trained on the target, and after that we altered course by five degrees every two minutes. The enemy's gun also appeared to be manned but it was still trained aft.

At 11:35, after closing slowly to 5,400 yards, the range suddenly began to open again. I ordered the guns to be loaded and turned fifteen degrees to starboard. I told the gunnery officer to unmask all guns but to use only the 7.5 cm and the two forward 6 inch for the first salvoes. As the camouflage flaps were raised we hoisted the German ensign and the flag signal denoting "heave-to." The enemy took no notice.

We could not believe that she had failed to observe the hoisting of flags and the unmasking of our guns; yet it was later established that in fact neither of these moves had been spotted nor had any of her crew become suspicious. Of course, as *Atlantis* was between her and the sun, she could see very little of us. When we saw that the enemy was steaming on without taking any notice, I altered twenty-five degrees away from her, thus bringing all our 6 inch guns to bear if required, and opened fire. The first salvo fell short and I wondered if it too had remained unobserved. The second salvo fell well ahead of the target and at last she turned away and my W/T office reported, "Enemy is sending distress signal. *LJUS Norwegian motorship Tirranna position . . .*" Our wireless began to jam hers by sending *"VVV test VVV"* but our secondary W/T office picked up the *Tirranna's* SOS several times before she ceased to transmit. By now the *Tirranna's* guns had definitely been manned and we could see it being trained. It fired one round which fell very short. Then our own guns roared again.

The Norwegian captain was not yet prepared to give in. He zigzagged so effectively between our salvoes that it was only with the sixth that we scored a hit. The *Tirranna* continued to dodge and we had to fire about one hundred and fifty rounds before she hove-to and hoisted a white flag. At this point the ships were still 8,200 yards apart—*Atlantis* had not gained a single yard throughout the engagement. I had given my gunnery officer a completely free hand and I was very pleased with his shooting; the fall of shot was well bunched and corrections were quickly and accurately set on. Three and a half hours after sighting her, we lay hove-to near our second victim. She was a 7,230-tonner built at Schichau in 1938 and was carrying a cargo of 3,000 tons of wheat and 27,000 sacks of flour for the British Ministry of Food, 6,000 bales of wool, 178 Army lorries and a load of canteen goods for the Australian troops in Palestine. She had been bound from Melbourne to Mombasa under Admiralty orders.

I sent the boarding party away under the command of the demolitions officer and accompanied as usual by my adjutant, Mohr. The *Tirranna* looked in poor shape; her crew were still on board as most of her lifeboats had been smashed. Jagged holes gaped in her upper works and amidships there was a sea of blood where a shell had ploughed through a group of stokers who had come up on deck. The holds and every available inch of deck space were crammed with lorries, cars and ambulances, many of them also badly damaged. The boarding party's first job was to transfer the wounded and I sent Captain Kamenz over with some reinforcements to assist them.

Gradually we pieced the story of the action together. The first round had hit just abaft the gun, the second struck the stern a few feet above the waterline, the third exploded near the radio cabin and the messspace below it, the fourth in the after part of the bridge; the fifth cut through a mast and penetrated the bridge structure before bursting on the foredeck, the sixth tore open the forward crew space. By contrast, the only damage sustained by the *Atlantis* was the buckling of two of the seaplane's floats by blast from our 6 inch guns.

The men off watch crowded to the ship's rail and stared curiously at the *Tirranna;* she was the first ship we had seen since the *Scientist.* Like *Atlantis,* she had been built in a German yard and was as large and as fast as the raider herself. Sub-Lieutenant Breuer, one of my prize officers, ordered the *Tirranna's* crew to pack their bags and stand by to transfer to *Atlantis.* It was Breuer who had procured a motorboat for us from the liner *Europa,* and this now proved particularly useful for the transfer of the wounded. With the exception of the chief and third engineers and one stoker, the whole crew were ferried across and accommodated separately from the *Scientist* prisoners.

The boarding party searched the *Tirranna* from truck to keelson. My senior Stoker CPO reported that the engines, gyro-compass and steering gear were all in order; the petty officer telegraphist checked on her radio and made a similar report, with the exception of the shattered wireless cabin. All damage could be repaired without difficulty.

Meanwhile the master of the *Tirranna,* Captain E. Hauff Gundersen, was sitting opposite Mohr and myself. Pale and still suffering from shock, but looking every inch a seaman as only a Norwegian can, he gave straight answers to our questions. When he told us that the *Tirranna* still had some 900 tons of fuel left, I compared this figure with the nature of the ship's cargo as reported by Captain Kamenz and saw at once that the ship was too valuable to be sunk, at any rate for the present.

The skipper also told us that he had left Oslo on February 18, 1940, and had sailed via the Atlantic, the Mediterranean and the Suez Canal for Ras Hafun in Italian Somaliland. From there he had taken a cargo of salt to Miri in Sarawak and thence had sailed on April 6 with oil for Hakodate in Japan. On arrival there he learned for the first time that war had broken out between Germany and Norway and at the same time received orders from the Norwegian consul to sail in ballast from Tokyo to Singapore, where he would receive a cargo and further orders from the British authorities. From May 1 to 14 the ship had lain in Sydney and from the 16th to the 29th in Melbourne. While in Melbourne she had been fitted with a 4.7 inch quick-firing gun on a platform and equipped with ammunition, smoke floats, gunnery-control telephone, a machine gun, rifles and steel helmets in accordance with the Regulations for Defensively Equipped Merchant Ships. Captain Gundersen said that his ship was the first armed Norwegian merchant ship to sail under the orders of the Australian Commonwealth's department of defense. She had loaded most of her cargo in Sydney, the rest—including the vehicles—in Melbourne, whence she had sailed for Mombasa on May 30.

All this information was subsequently confirmed from papers that the master had torn up and put in the bridge wastepaper basket, and which we carefully pieced together again. The results of this labor were indeed rewarding; from it we learned, for example, that the chief controller of shipping at Melbourne had assured Captain Gundersen that he could sleep peacefully in his bunk as far as Mombasa, since there were no German warships in the Indian Ocean; but that he would have to watch out for mines laid by the pocket-battleship *Graf Spee* off Cape Agulhas. I was glad to hear of this officially sponsored untruth as it meant that in future none of our victims would suspect our harmless-looking freighter of having laid those mines.

"Why did you paint your ship so dark and erase her name from bow and stern?" I asked.

"On orders from the Norwegian consul," Gundersen answered. "We bought some dark paint and changed her color while at sea."

We also learned that most of the cargo, including eight hundred bags of mail, was destined for the British Army in Palestine and that there were a lot of ships loading war supplies in Australian ports. Added to what the master of the *Scientist* had said, this confirmed my belief that the British were directing a part of their shipping across the Pacific and through the Panama Canal, whence the ships were sailed in convoy across the Atlantic. As such a long detour involved more time at sea, higher charges and a slower turnaround, it was clear that the British still had plenty of ships to be able to afford it. But they obviously would not have done this if it could have been avoided, so it seemed as though our raider warfare was beginning to pay dividends.

It was hard to make the Norwegian master understand that he had lost his fine ship for ever. "But peace has been signed between Norway and Germany, Captain," he said with tears in his eyes. "I never knew your ship was a raider. I said to my chief engineer, 'That Dutchman is making good speed but we won't let him pass us,' and so we went up to full speed to see if you were faster than we were. All my officers and I thought you were one of the 'kerk' class."

"Yes," broke in the chief engineer, "when and where did you capture the *Abbekerk?*" He still thought he was on board a Dutch ship and when he learned that the *"Abbekerk"* was really the *Goldenfels,* he said, "I'd never have believed it." I did not know then that one year before—in peacetime—the *Goldenfels* and the *Tirranna* were berthed close to each other in Bombay and a football match had been arranged between the two crews.

"Why didn't you stop," I asked, "when we hoisted our ensign and flag signal? Why didn't you at least stop when we opened fire?"

"We never saw your flags," Gundersen replied with a shrug. "Your ship was between us and the sun. And later—would *you* have stopped when your ship could do seventeen knots?"

I had nothing to say to that, for of course I should have done the same.

"Are you going to shoot me?" asked Gundersen after a long silence. "Perhaps I have deserved it for being so stupid." He wiped the sweat off his face with the back of his hand and looked at me anxiously. "What have I done? Five of my men are dead and I am to blame."

"Don't worry, Captain Gundersen," I said soothingly. "No one is going to hurt you. It's sad enough that you have had such heavy losses. I would like to offer you my sympathy and that of my men."

The Norwegian nodded silently, his face drawn with grief. His crew were as upset as their captain. They stood huddled together on deck, terrified lest we should put them back in the boats and cast them adrift. They only lost their fears when they saw that they were going to remain on board the raider; then they went willingly to their new quarters.

Despite the superficial damage she had sustained, the *Tirranna* was perfectly seaworthy and I decided to send her off with a prize crew to wait in a remote position. Later I would have to decide whether to sink her or send her home through the blockade. Meanwhile we could replenish our stores from her cargo. The *Tirranna* had plenty of good things on board—beer, tobacco, tinned peaches, marmalade, soap, chocolate, hams and cheeses. She also carried some secret papers which her officers had been unable to destroy— routing orders from Melbourne to Mombasa, sailing certificates from the Australian Navy, regulations for armed merchant ships, gunnery tables, supply notes for defensive equipment and handbooks on gunnery and gun maintenance. She was able to spare one hundred tons of oil for the *Atlantis,* assuming that she could replenish her supplies before sailing for home as a prize. All night long the oil was pumped from the *Tirranna*'s bunkers into ours, while the working parties' boats shuttled back and forth between the ships. On the morning of June 12 the *Tirranna* sailed off to her rendezvous manned by twelve Germans, seven Norwegians and eight Lascars.

Before she left I sent for Sub-Lieutenant (S) Waldmann, her new master, to give him his instructions. Having offered him a cigarette and told him to sit down, I outlined my plans. If we succeeded in capturing a ship with full fuel tanks, I would send her to refuel the *Tirranna,* which would then sail for home. "At the moment," I said, "the *Tirranna* has two hundred and fifty tons of oil on board, of which you will be using five tons a day at the most. By lying hove-to at the rendezvous you can cut your consumption to half a ton, so we can reckon that you can last out until August 30 without difficulty. You have plenty of food and water on board and you can also break into the cargo. Now, as to the waiting positions. Up to August 1, remain in position 31°10′S, 68°30′E. If you are sighted, move to an evasion position at 32° 40′S, 71°E. If you are not in touch with us by August 1, steer for position 33°30′S, 68°10′E and wait for us there until the 31." I told him to retain the ship's identity; if he was stopped, he was to try to avert suspicion by pretending that he had been chased and fired on but had escaped with the loss of his captain, the destruction of his radio, and so on. If a boarding party were sent over, he was to scuttle the ship and take to the boats. I had provided him with a spare lifeboat to replace the *Tirranna*'s damaged ones.

Waldmann repeated these orders and left to take charge of our first prize. A few minutes later both ships were once more under way, leaving behind them nothing but a patch of oil and a few planks and empty boxes floating on the water.

7

THE *CITY OF BAGHDAD*

We steamed back through stormy weather toward the shipping lanes, adjusting speed to reach them at dawn. Assuming that ships would be moving north or south of the course steered by the *Tirranna,* I planned to steam in shallow zigzags along the route in an easterly direction. Once the loss of the *Tirranna* became known, the length of time we could stay in these waters would depend largely upon how soon the raider *Orion* made her presence felt off Australia, for by doing so she would provide *Atlantis* with a perfect alibi and give us a chance of pursuing our activities in the north without fear of interruption.

The disappearance of the seventeen-knot *Tirranna* was bound to create a lot of problems for the enemy, especially as there could be so many solutions to the mystery. The *Daily Telegraph,* for example, had said that the German aircraft carrier *Graf Zeppelin* was operating in the South Atlantic; this carrier did not in fact exist—building had begun on her just before war broke out and no progress had been made since then. This sort of report revealed the enemy's nervous state of mind.

On the afternoon of June 13 I mustered the ship's company. There was a lot that I wanted to say to them, in particular things that I had noticed during the searching of the *Tirranna.* Some of the ratings had appropriated souvenirs right under the noses of the Norwegians. It was understandable, I said, that each man should want a keepsake, but such things must be kept within reasonable proportions and for the future I laid down strict regulations on the "requisitioning" of such mementoes, clearly defining the difference between legitimate spoils and plain loot; any breach of the new regulations would, I warned, be punished with the utmost rigor. I further decreed that each and every object found on board a captured ship might only be removed with the permission of an officer and against a receipt issued by me.

Day after day we steamed back along the *Tirranna*'s tracks, but the seas remained empty. While we were waiting we spent the time repainting the ship to make her resemble a Norwegian or Dutch vessel sailing under British orders. There was no point in trying to make her look exactly like a British ship as they all had a gun mounted aft on a very distinctive platform. I thought it was more practical to give the ship a darker overall color like that of the *Tirranna* and to add Norwegian markings roughly painted over in such a way that they could only just be seen. We also darkened the upper works, leaving only the top masts light-colored; dark topmasts had caused the downfall of many a ship, including the *Tirranna* herself.

On June 16 we abandoned our search and steered for the intersection of the Australia-Aden and Sunda Strait-Durban routes. This endless waiting and inactivity was taxing everyone's nerves. In France the German armies were rolling westward; the news from the German overseas radio sounded as though the war would be over in twenty-four hours. My ship's company were impatient for another victory; they could see no point in hanging around in these godforsaken waters while at home the fate of Europe was being decided. The men were laying bets on how long the war would last, now that France had been beaten to her knees. The younger they were the shorter time they reckoned to the end of the war, and the older sailors—especially those who had fought in the First World War—shook their heads cautiously. "Britain's sea power is still intact," they said. "France may have been knocked out but England hasn't even been bruised yet—and there is still America to be reckoned with."

I called a conference of the navigating officer, the chief engineer, the administrative officer and Mohr to see how long we could remain at sea. Flour, butter, sugar, water, oil and mileage were the deciding factors. It was now necessary to economize more than ever. The war would last longer than people thought—of that I was sure. To save fuel I frequently stopped engines and allowed the ship to drift. At last came news of the raider *Orion;* the liner *Niagara* of 13,000 tons had been sunk off Auckland. The idea of *Atlantis* also operating off a coast was attractive, but I stuck to my original plans.

The days went by with the same monotonous routine—on watch; off watch; deck watch; engine watch; training routine; cleaning down paintwork; scraping rust; checking torpedoes; baking bread; cooking; peeling potatoes; mending shoes; tending the sick; taking turns at the wheel; fixing our position; exercises; instruction; washing clothes; "cooks to the galley" and all the rest of it. And every day at noon the same entry in the log: "Nothing sighted."

Every forenoon my first lieutenant went on his early morning rounds of the ship. As soon as the boatswain had detailed the men for the day's work, Kühn would come up to the bridge to be briefed on our position. He would have a word with the navigator, the officer of the watch and the chief coxswain, give a cheery nod to the lookouts, take a hand in fixing our position and then go forward through the aircraft hangar in No. 2 hold to the capstan, where he would peer down at both sides of the ship to see whether our camouflage paint was being betrayed by any telltale streaks of rust. Then he would make his way back to the sick bay, to exchange a few words with the doctors and their patients, and move on to the forward guns, passing through one of the magazines and so through the shipwrights' and paint shop to the small prisoners' quarters one deck down. On his way back he would walk past the forward gun crew's quarters to reach the air crew's space and their workshops. Up again to the boat deck where he would look over the ship's boats;

here we had installed a children's nursery and he always stopped to watch these youngest of our prisoners playing under their mothers' watchful eye. On again to the chief engineer and then to the coal bunkers and iron ration stores, the shoemaker's shop, the bakery and galley, the steering compartment, isolation hospital, mine space and lastly the after gun on the poop.

By eleven o'clock he was usually back in his cabin, where the divisional officers were waiting for him with their reports; but there were some days when he would crawl into the furthest corner of the engine room and check up on every piece of machinery he could reach. My first lieutenant was nothing if not thorough.

From time to time intelligence reports came in which helped us to assess the general situation. The naval staff announced that Dutch East Indian ports were extinguishing harbor lights; it was assumed in Berlin that this was due to minelaying operations off New Zealand but I put it down to the disappearance of the *Tirranna,* of which Berlin was still in ignorance. Then an unknown British radio station sent a message *en clair* to a Dutch ship with instructions on the course to be steered in the Sunda Strait. From this we deduced that Dutch ships were not yet in possession of British code books. Three weeks were to elapse before our next encounter with an enemy, but during all that time, when it seemed as though the outcome of the war was being decided on the continent of Europe, we were left almost without any official news from the German Admiralty. It looked as though Berlin had assumed that *Atlantis* could no longer receive transmissions from Germany; all the fateful news about the fall of France reached us from Indian, Australian and Japanese stations. Curiously enough, San Francisco relayed the news bulletin of the German overseas service before the German short-wave station did; even the news of the cessation of hostilities in France reached us by this route. We held a thanksgiving service on board on the afternoon of June 25.

Several shore stations were now calling the *Tirranna,* including Colombo, Mombasa and Hong Kong;

but the *Tirranna* of course could not answer and *Atlantis* was certainly not going to make imaginary signals in her name—it might be that the enemy was waiting for her to do just that. Captain Gundersen was heard to say miserably, "The people in Australia will say that I belong to the Fifth Column and have decamped with my ship to Vladivostok or Japan." He was obviously much upset at the thought of being unjustly suspected.

I saw to it that my officers' relations with our prisoners were correct but friendly. The merchant skippers formed a club among themselves and spent their time reading, playing cards or chess or just chatting. Occasionally one of them could be seen taking a turn on deck with one of my officers and sometimes in the evening they held a small party to which they would invite Mohr, Dr. Reil and myself. Stimulated by whiskey and soda, the talk would range around the world and we could almost forget the existence of war and the fact that they and we belonged to opposite sides. The club's membership changed as time went on; older members were shipped home in prizes and their place was taken by new ones. But I was pleased to find that the original clublike atmosphere of mutual respect was never allowed to disappear. There seemed nothing incongruous in the way in which one member—a crusty seadog of the old school—would muster his crew daily for divine worship, praying regularly and fearlessly for the appearance of a British cruiser to blow *Atlantis* out of the water.

On July 2 we made a sortie toward the Sunda Strait-Mauritius route in the direction of the Cocos Islands, hoping to find a tanker carrying oil from Miri, but once again we drew blank. During this period of fruitless search I was reminded of how Admiral Jellicoe had written that "victory depends less upon the stimulant of success than upon the patient performance of one's duty by day and night and in all weathers." Commander Nerger had echoed this sentiment when he wrote, "It is more difficult to endure patiently than to attack courageously."

On July 10 we had got within six hundred miles of Colombo and at dawn the next day we turned westward to cover our patrol area once more. And then at last came that which we had been waiting for—a smoke cloud.

It was 6:43 A.M.; the smoke was so thick that at first we thought it must be coming from several ships together. I cleared for action and stopped engines—their vibrations made it difficult to train binoculars on the target. Then we lay and waited, trying to pierce the morning haze, from which all that appeared at first was a thin pair of masts on either side of the thick pall of smoke. The ship came slowly over the horizon, paying no attention to us, who by that time were under way again. I ordered the second engine to be started and the ship brought to full speed as soon as possible. (The diesels could not be run at high speed straightaway because the temperature of the water was too high.) As our speed gradually increased we turned unobtrusively toward the enemy, which was becoming easier to see every minute as she emerged from the haze: we could soon make out that she had one funnel, a dark-colored hull and dirty brown upper works. She carried no nationality markings but as she cruised unsuspectingly across our bows 7,500 yards away, we could see that she was armed with the usual gun on a platform aft—that meant that she was British.

"But by her build I should say that she was originally German," said Sub-Lieutenant Mund, who had been first mate of the *Goldenfels,* "Hansa Line, I should think."

On the advice of my radio officer I delayed my attack until after the routine period for distress signals, during which there was radio silence all over the world. Once that was past, we raised the camouflage flaps and fired four warning shots from the 7.5 cm gun. Our ensign and flag signal to heave-to streamed out in the breeze. Although the ship acknowledged the flag signal she at once began to use her radio. She got as far as "*QQQQ—shelled by ra . . .*" when a direct hit in the radio room put an end to her distress signal and another shattered the mast; at the same time we started up our jamming transmitter, using corrupt Japanese call signs. Then we ceased fire.

The incident had not gone unnoticed. The American s.s. *Eastern Guide* radioed, *"Who shelled by . . . ?"*

"QRU" came our reply brusquely, *"I have nothing for you."*

But the *Eastern Guide* was still suspicious. *"Stop transmitting,"* she signaled to us, *"Who shelled by . . . ?"* She was answered, not by *Atlantis* but by a shore station which repeated *"QRU"* several times, after which there was silence.

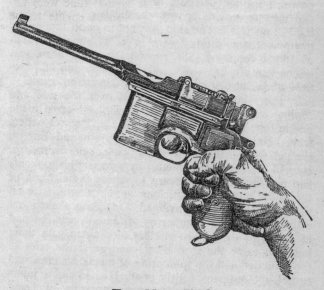

Heavy Mauser Pistol

Our victim's fate was sealed. Instead of obeying our orders to remain on board, her crew were hastily abandoning ship. The same panicky flight to the boats occurred in every ship, and always for the same reason —the malevolence of the Allied Press which had instilled into the enemy a fear of being murdered by the straight for the chart room and officers' cabins, arriving

Germans; they felt it was better to face an unknown fate in an open boat than to be captured by German pirates.

When our boarding party reached the ship they found that Mund had been right; she was originally the 7,506-ton *Geierfels,* built at Tecklenborg in 1919 and later handed over to England under the terms of the Treaty of Versailles. Now the property of the Ellerman Line and renamed the *City of Baghdad,* she was bound from England to Penang. Her cargo consisted of coke, steel tubes, railway lines and steel bars—some destined for the defences of Singapore—paint, artificial manure, engine spares, chemicals and whiskey—9,324 tons in all. The ship was not in good shape; her equipment and fittings were in short supply and in neglected condition. She carried the usual armament —one gun aft, 2 cm AA and a 4.7 inch gun of Japanese make, also smoke floats and degaussing cable.

The boarding party swarmed over the side and Mohr, carrying a heavy Mauser pistol, as usual made just in time to prevent some of the ship's secret papers from being destroyed. The tall, white-haired English skipper was on the point of throwing them overboard. He had been taken completely by surprise; his lookouts had not thought it necessary to report the sighting of the raider and their suspicions were not aroused even when the two ships converged. On being shaken out of his well-earned slumber by *Atlantis's* guns, he had at first tried to use his wireless, hoping to gain time; but then came the shell bursts and amid the cries of the wounded and the splintering of metal, his crew had rushed in blind panic for the boats. He had had to intervene to prevent the boats from capsizing or being smashed against the side, and thus lost so much time that he could not destroy his papers. Pistol in hand, Mohr informed him politely in English that he must regard himself as a prisoner; realizing that further resistance was useless, the Englishman obeyed Mohr's summons to go on deck. There he found his crew— who had been brought back on board by my men— busy collecting their belongings before being transferred to *Atlantis*. He and his officers were invited to do the same.

The boarding party was hard at work. Sacks full of things both practical and pleasant lay heaped next to very welcome supplies of fresh potatoes taken from the *City of Baghdad*'s holds, while stocks of rice were loaded into the boats for our Indian prisoners. The scuttling party soon had their charges in place and just after midday the boarding party left the ship with the last of the British prisoners, leaving only the demolition party on board. Lieutenant Fehler, who had been very dissatisfied with the results of his efforts to sink the *Scientist,* had decided not only to increase his charges to 260 lbs. (160 lbs. would have been ample) but to watch results on the spot. The demolition party waited until the charges had gone off—"and the explosion was not so bad as the waiting," they said—and reached their boat only just in time before the *City of Baghdad* began to sink by the stern. Fehler himself cut things so fine that he ripped his arm open jumping into the boat and I had to reprimand him for taking unnecessary risks.

We now had to find room for eighty-one new prisoners—twenty-one whites and sixty Lascars. Two of the English were wounded—the boatswain had lost a foot and the W/T operator had been miraculously dragged alive from his shattered cabin, suffering only superficial wounds to his arms.

As soon as the *City of Baghdad* had sunk we steamed off at high speed. I had chosen a southerly course on the assumption that it would be the last direction in which the enemy would look for a raider; it was almost certain that the master of the *Eastern Guide* would make a report at his next port of call and in any case it was as well to withdraw from an area which the enemy would soon be starting to search. Our new course would enable us to cover the routes from Australia and the Sunda Strait to Mombasa and Aden, and from South Africa to Mauritius and Rangoon.

During the afternoon I summoned all officers to a

conference to analyze the engagement and to discover what lessons could be learned from it. At the outset of the action we had had a failure in the steering gear which threw the ship out of control for two minutes. This was one of the risks that had to be run; we could not ensure with 100 per cent certainty against a repetition of the failure. I commended the W/T officer for his advice on delaying the attack until after the routine time for SOS signals. I gave orders that in future all drifting liferafts were to be secured, to prevent anyone from swimming over to them; anyone doing so might be overlooked and not picked up. I also said that dead bodies on the enemy ship were to be carried below straight away, so that the work of the search parties should not be carried on all around them. We would thus ensure proper respect for the dead and spare the feelings of the survivors. I told the gunnery officer that in future he was to fire two warning shots from the 6 inch guns. The 7.5 cm did not make as big an impression as the roar and impact of the heavier caliber, and it would give the gunnery officer an earlier opportunity of gauging the range and thus destroying the enemy's wireless sooner.

Among the secret papers collected from the *City of Baghdad* was one of particular importance—a description of the raider based on reports from the *City of Exeter,* entitled "Report of a Suspicious Vessel." Two photographs of the Hansa Line's *Freienfels* were attached and there followed a description of "a ship sighted in the South Atlantic on May 2, 1940" which coincided in every detail with the *Atlantis.* The *City of Exeter* had smelled a rat. I decided to alter the appearance of the ship as far as possible by fitting further gallow masts fore and aft; we could make them out of empty barrels, of which there were plenty on board. In an interview with Captain Armstrong White, master of the *City of Baghdad,* it transpired that he had paid little attention to the *City of Exeter*'s report. There had, he pointed out, been no mention in it of a raider; "a suspicious-looking ship" could just as well be a merchant ship running the gauntlet of the Allied blockade. Such ships were known to have got through successfully, though some were known to have been captured or to have been scuttled. In any case, he said, the report came from the South Atlantic and was over two months old. Who would expect such a description to hold good after such a long time? Captain White told me that, in accordance with instructions, he had steered in shallow zigzags at dawn and dusk and in foggy weather, and had changed his course each day. He had sailed in convoy from Gibraltar, and had rounded the Cape outside the 100-fathom-line; he had heard rumors in Lourenço Marques of the appearance of a raider in the Indian Ocean but that had sounded like local gossip and was so vague that he had paid no attention to it.

From all this it was clear to me that the enemy had no real idea as to our position or even as to our existence. I resolved to take no further evasive action to the south and accordingly shaped course to the westward again.

8

THE *KEMMENDINE*'S GUNNER

"Smoke to port!" Two lookouts gave the alarm at the same moment. It was 9:34 A.M., Saturday, July 13. Above the misty horizon hung a tenuous dark thread; below it emerged the ship's funnel and masts, and then her upper works. If she were keeping as sharp a lookout as ourselves, the must have already sighted *Atlantis*. To avert suspicion, and incidentally to gain a tactical advantage, I turned 20 degrees to starboard; just then the W/T office reported loud tuning noises from a transmitter in the vicinity. The enemy ship was clearly about to send a signal.

I told the gunnery officer not to waste time firing warning shots. "When I tell you to open fire, use every gun that will bear and destroy the enemy's wireless!" As Kasch acknowledged my order, I rang down for speed to be reduced from nine to seven knots. The enemy ship—a large one—held on her course unsuspectingly, only turning sufficiently to pass astern of us in accordance with the international rule of the road. We turned slowly and unobtrusively with her, to reduce the range which was still considerable. The enemy gave no sign of having noticed this and the range began to decrease. At 10:09 the range was down to 5,400; we dropped our disguise and opened fire.

The first four salvoes fell wide of the mark but shells from the fifth and sixth hit the target. The bridge burst into flames. One shell tore a hole just above the waterline, a second hit below the bridge and a third exploded in the port boiler room and pierced a steam pipe.

"Is the enemy transmitting?" I asked several times, but each time came the answer, "No." Then the other ship hoisted flag K—"I am stopping"—and we ceased fire. Our surprise attack had succeeded perfectly and the enemy was surrendering docilely without using her radio. We steamed slowly up to the enemy's stern. Through our glasses we could see that the boats had been manned and launched and even now were rowing over toward us; our camouflage flaps were once more in place and our boarding party was standing by to go over to the captured ship. Everything was proceeding according to plan. I could now read the other ship's name, *Kemmendine;* with her ample passenger accommodation she was obviously well suited to be sent back home with the prisoners as a blockade runner—always provided that she had enough fuel—but first the fire on her bridge had to be put out and the damaged steam pipe patched up.

My thoughts were rudely interrupted when a gun went off and a shell screamed over the bridge. The *Kemmendine* had opened fire—nine minutes after surrendering, when her boats were already moving toward us and a signal asking for medical aid was flying from her yardarm! I shouted to Kasch to open fire and ordered full speed ahead. The camouflage flaps shot up again and seconds later the British ship's stern lay under a murderous fire. I could see a lone figure standing by her gun, but as soon as we returned his fire, he dashed away from it, and we promptly ceased fire again. I was seething with rage and swore I could court-martial the idiotic culprit.

We found out later that the ship's master himself was not to blame; a single gunner had deliberately disregarded his orders and pulled the lanyard of the loaded gun. In civil life—and for some reason my anger faded when I heard this—he was a London window cleaner; it was lucky for him that his thoughtless action had not led to greater loss of life and limb. That he had forced us to waste valuable time was bad enough; but worse still, the *Kemmendine* was now so badly shot up that she could not be saved. Her bridge was one glowing mass—to board her and lay scuttling charges was out of the question. A column of black smoke was billowing up from her that would rouse the suspicions of any passing ship, so we had to use torpedoes to sink her.

The first torpedo failed to run at its set depth and struck the *Kemmendine* amidships on the waterline; the second also hit her too high. But in the heavy swell the ship broke in two, the halves rearing up on end for a moment before, slowly at first and then ever more quickly, they sank in a confused and eddying mass of debris.

The survivors who had reached the deck of *Atlantis* and those still in the boats watched with ashen faces as their ship went down, then turned dumbly to look at us. The *Kemmendine* had belonged to the British India-Burma Line; she was a 7,769-ton ship built in Glasgow in 1924. She had worn a wartime coat of brown paint on her upper works with gray masts, black funnel without markings and a black hull relieved only by the yellow cross denoting that she had been degaussed. She had been bound for Glasgow via Gibraltar and Capetown for Rangoon. Her master boarded us in company with twenty-six white officers and men, eighty-six Lascars, seven white passengers consisting of five women and two children, and twenty-eight Indian passengers. According to her master, her cargo had consisted only of small quantities of beer and whiskey.

The women, who were promptly placed in the care of my PMO, were the wives of British officials in Burma, while among the Asiatics were several merchants and their families who had been evacuated from Gibraltar. Although they had lost their entire possessions in the *Kemmendine*—chests of silks, carpets, jewelry and ornaments—they smiled and retained perfect composure in keeping with their religious precepts. As high caste members of a different faith they were placed in an isolation ward to keep them separate from the other prisoners and given their own cooking facilities.

As soon as the *Kemmendine*'s crew and passengers had been transferred, her boats were drenched with petrol and set on fire but the petrol evaporated before the flames really caught; the boats had to be shot to pieces with the 7.5 cm and AA guns until all traces of them had vanished. We noticed that each boat was provided with a lead container which held up-to-date information on the course and distance to the nearest coast—in this case Colombo and Sumatra.

That afternoon, while we were steaming away from the scene of the sinking, I convened a formal inquiry to establish the sequence of events on board the *Kemmendine* after she had hoisted the "K" signal. This was essential lest we should subsequently be accused of firing on open boats. Such in fact was the case, until Captain Armstrong White of the *City of Baghdad* scotched the rumor by issuing a flat contradiction of it. The court of inquiry consisted of myself, Captain Kamenz, Lieutenant Mohr and the master (Captain R. B. Reid) and first mate of the *Kemmendine*. It transpired that the noise of steam escaping from the damaged pipe had drowned the master's order to abandon the gun. At the same time as he hoisted the "K" flag he had stopped engines and given orders to abandon ship; he had not noticed the firing of the gun and learned of it only when I told him. These findings were set down on paper and signed by Captain Reid with Captain Armstrong White as witness.

Long afterward we learned of the deep impression made on India and Burma by the sinking of the *Kemmendine* and the unknown fate of her passengers and crew. Not only were many of her passengers related to high officials, but the ship herself was equally well known. This was the first time that a German commerce raider had directly influenced Indian public opinion; a Burmese newspaper editor expressed the country's feelings when he wrote that "the loss of this ship has cast a shadow over the whole of Burma."

9

A FAMILY CONCERN

On the evening of July 13 I mustered all hands and gave a talk on the events of the 11th and 13th. At its close I announced that thirty Second Class Iron Crosses had been awarded to the ship for services rendered up to July 10. However, in order to prevent jealousy—and because we had no medals on board anyway—I decreed that the conferring of the actual awards would be postponed until the ship returned home or further awards were made. Since every man had done his duty, I said, these awards might be regarded as recognition of the services rendered by all; they should be an incentive to further achievement. I reminded the men once again of the strict orders against looting; at the same time I promised that a regular issue of "souvenirs" would be made in due course to each man and in such a way that everyone would receive something, whether he served in the boarding party or as a stoker below decks.

Up to the sinking of the *Kemmendine*—three and a half months after leaving Germany—I had not made a single signal; unlike the other raiders I had kept strict wireless silence. Being well aware of my reluctance to use radio, the Naval Staff had not worried unduly about my ship, deducing correctly from reports of the Agulhas minefield and from various signals from the British Admiralty that my silence was deliberate. On the other hand *Atlantis* had been the first raider to put to sea and Berlin was badly in need of information particularly about the Indian Ocean, which the German radio intelligence service had difficulty in covering. On June 8 I had been ordered to make a signal reporting my position and sinkings to date. Raider warfare was a new field of operations for everyone concerned in it and *Atlantis,* as the first raider, was looked upon as a pioneer; the Naval Staff in Berlin expected me to use the permission granted me to send short messages.

When five weeks had gone by without any news from us, Berlin repeated the order, adding that this was a matter of urgency and that—according to reports made by the *Graf Spee*—we stood in little danger of being D/F'd (located by the enemy's radio direction finders.) I accordingly made my first signal on July 14 thus: *"6°S, 77°E, can endure for more than 85 days, 30,000 tons sunk to date."*

But neither this signal nor a repetition of it sent two days later was received in Berlin, although we could pick up Berlin's transmissions at strength 4 to 5. The text of the signal eventually arrived three weeks later by a roundabout route.

For the next few days we zigzagged once more over our original search area. Berlin had reported that a convoy of troop transports had sailed from Singapore and would pass close to us on about the twentieth—this we had at all costs to avoid. At dusk we steamed southward, keeping to a steady thirteen knots during the night and only dropping down to nine knots when morning came. It was best to be on the safe side. On each day thereafter we tried to send our signal, but without success. At last we even sent the message on Berlin's own transmitting wave, to see if it would be interrupted, but nothing happened. Next day we sent out our call sign twice at intervals of an hour, well before it would be dawn in Germany. The only result was that two days later Berlin reported that the W/T intercepting staff of the British Commander-in-Chief, East Indies, had taken radio bearings from which an enemy auxiliary cruiser was estimated to be in latitude 5°30′ south, longitude unknown. Soon after this came a signal from Berlin that the British Admiralty had warned all shipping in home waters to make an immediate report on any ship that looked suspicious, and to regard any vessel that approached them as a raider, so that the enemy would have less time to destroy their aerials.

It seemed curious to me that this order should only apply to ships in home waters and not to those in the Indian Ocean or elsewhere.

It was about this time that two of my wireless operators, Wentzel and Wesemann, scored a remarkable success. Wesemann had served for three years in the German decryption service, deciphering foreign messages. He now succeeded in deciphering large portions of the British merchant navy code, solely on the basis of two complete signals picked up separately. Using the groups of the two signals as key indicators and setting them alongside the possible meanings of subsequent intercepts, he gradually put together about one-third of the groups in the British transposition table No. 1 for the merchant navy code; this was of inestimable value to me, as I was henceforth able to read the greater part of the British W/T traffic.

Another signal received from Berlin decreed that all French ships on the high seas were to be treated as hostile, while the laws regarding prizes and contraband were to be enforced in respect of cargoes destined for Unoccupied France and French possessions. It naturally followed that the areas around such territories were to be regarded as enemy waters. Next came an announcement from Berlin that the waters off Cape St. Francis in South Africa had been allocated to "Ship 33"—the raider *Pinguin*—for minelaying. I found this order very confusing and I tried to work out Berlin's line of reasoning. We could easily have mined Cape St. Francis at the same time as Cape Agulhas, and the second minefield might still not have been identified. Apart from the danger to the *Pinguin* there seemed to be no point in laying mines inside the 100-fathom-line when all Allied ships had been warned to keep outside it. Furthermore the appearance of the *Pinguin* on the scene would be very embarrassing to us; there was not only the chance of her operational area in the Indian Ocean overlapping with ours, but danger also lay in the similarity between the two raiders—both of them had originally been Hansa Line ships.

This was not my only headache at the time. The unending stream of wireless messages that we intercepted showed that the raider *Widder* had caused a sensation by sinking two ships within the so-called American Security Zone and leaving the survivors adrift in their open boats. Only a month previously both the *Atlantis* and *Orion* had been warned by signal to respect this zone. After the *Widder*'s activities in the Caribbean the question arose whether there had been any change in policy of which the *Atlantis* and *Orion* had been left in ignorance.

We steamed for two days more along the *Tirranna*'s route before shaping course toward the *Tirranna* herself. At 7:22 A.M. on July 29 we sighted her at the rendezvous and lost no time in transferring fuel and stores. I had decided to sail the *Tirranna* for home as soon as she had refueled and replenished; *Atlantis* would then begin her first major overhaul and at the same time take the opportunity of carrying out a number of smaller repairs. Motor boats and cutters shuttled back and forth incessantly between the two ships while *Atlantis*'s engine room staff began their overhaul; this was no easy matter in the tropical heat, but Kielhorn's men set to work with a will.

I realized that the first phase of my campaign had come to an end. It had been successful despite the difficulty of locating enemy ships sailing independently over such a vast area of sea. Most important of all, the enemy had had no idea of the extent of our operational area, so long as we remained in it. Although the enemy could have deduced our position by working back from the *City of Baghdad*'s known course and last transmission, they would still not know whether *Atlantis* was a U-boat or a surface ship. The number of signals passing to and from the commander-in-chief, East Indies, indicated that there was much anxiety in his command and that he had very little idea of our whereabouts. Reports that we had received of small craft patroling off Aden might well have something to do with this. By contrast, our experiences had taught us a lot about the countermeasures and precautions being adopted by the British; we had learned that the masters and crews of enemy ships were less alert when on the high seas than in coastal waters. We also realized that in the future we would have more time to carry out repairs to our prizes, and to transfer stores from them; while from what we had learned from captured documents we now knew that we could operate nearer the coast and in more frequented waters without fear of counterattack.

As soon as we had transferred the prisoners and made the *Tirranna* ready to sail, I decided to shape course toward Madagascar and Mauritius. The transfer of 420 tons of diesel oil to the *Tirranna* would materially lessen our endurance, on the other hand it was imperative that we should rid ourselves of nearly four hundred prisoners who were no less of a problem since they were making big inroads into our food supplies. In any case the alternative of sinking the *Tirranna* was out of the question as her cargo was so valuable.

Fueling the *Tirranna* was no easy matter as a sudden storm had blown up with wind force 7, sea force 4 and a heavy swell. In order to save time, *Atlantis* and her prize were placed one astern of the other and connected by strong manila hawsers. Unfortunately the rear ship was constantly crowding up toward the stern of the other: and the working of propellers to rectify this put such a strain on the two nine-inch hawsers that they parted abruptly after only 45 tons of oil had been transferred, and refueling had to be stopped. The two ships lay hove-to throughout the night and despite continuing heavy seas, wind and rain, the transfer of supplies was resumed next morning.

A new method of fueling had been carefully worked out for me on paper by Captain Kamenz. Both ships steamed very slowly ahead at a short distance from each other, while a motor boat brought a three inch line from one to the other; to this was attached a seven inch rope hawser and to that again a six inch steel towing wire, and so connection was reestablished. A fuel pipe was connected up between the two ships independently of the towing wire and they then both steamed at slow speed on slightly converging courses until the towing ship could take the strain; the towed ship then stopped her engines and remained at a steady distance from the other with lightly loaded hawsers. In this way 450 tons of diesel oil were transferred from the *Atlantis* to the *Tirranna* in three and a half hours. With a total of 650 tons of fuel the *Tirranna* could easily reach one of the ports in the Bay of Biscay.

Just as we were completing the transfer of supplies, Mohr discovered a grave misdemeanor on the part of the *Tirranna*'s prize crew. Led by a CPO telegraphist, the entire crew had broken into the mailbags and rifled their contents; the telegraphist alone had taken enough to stock a shop. As soon as the prize's captain discovered what was going on, he ordered it to be stopped and everything tidied up, allowing each man to keep three pairs of socks, two shirts and a pullover; but despite the strictest orders against the retention of anything else, Mohr found that between them the eleven members of the prize crew had kept several things for themselves. I immediately ordered the men to be court-martialed—but that was not all. Shortly before this a pair of binoculars belonging to the master of the *City of Baghdad* had disappeared. An appeal to the crew's sense of honor produced no result but a note was found in a locker to the effect that the thief had thrown the glasses overboard to avoid detection. A comparison of handwriting led to the exposure of the guilty man—a bosun's mate—who duly confessed. A court-martial presided over by Mohr, with Bulla and the boatswain as members, condemned him to two years' imprisonment, dishonorable discharge from the Navy and the payment of compensation to Captain Armstrong White. He was ordered to be shipped home in our next prize.

After working hard for four and a half days, the aircraft maintenance crew managed to assemble an aircraft from the spare parts on board. Although they had no written instructions to guide them, they succeeded in building a machine that flew. On its first flight, carrying 45 gallons of petrol but no armament, it made a couple of sweeps around the ship and landed safely. In the afternoon it took off again, with less fuel but with machine guns mounted and carrying two 110-lb. bombs.

As repairs to the *Atlantis*'s engines were proceeding satisfactorily, I was able to turn my attention to the transfer of the prisoners—the women and children and Indian passengers first, then the British and Norwegians. I also put a party of ratings under Lieutenant Fehler on board the *Tirranna* to expedite repairs. Both ships freshened up their paintwork, restowed cargo, chipped rust and overhauled gear. Work proceeded uneventfully in the calm weather and at noon on Friday, August 2 the usual entry, "Nothing sighted," was about to be written up in the log when a ship suddenly emerged out of the haze.

The *Tirranna* was the first to sight her and blew her siren to attract our attention. In a flash *Atlantis* was transformed into a hive of activity. Men stumbled over each other, alarm bells shrilled, orders were shouted in a medley of voices, the engine-room telegraphs clanged and we worked up to full speed to give ourselves room to maneuver. The enemy ship was approaching at high speed. We learned later that the reason for this suspicious behavior was a very human one —curiosity on the part of the ship's second officer, who was on watch at the time. He thought he had come upon a rendezvous between two sister ships and later, on sighting the boats plying between them, he assumed that one of the ships had engine trouble.

As *Atlantis* gathered way the ratings on the stages

hanging over her sides hurriedly clambered back on board with their paint pots and brushes and raced to their action stations; a solitary seaman in a tiny dinghy rowed desperately after us, fearful of being abandoned in the Indian Ocean. The *Tirranna,* with a part of *Atlantis*'s crew still on board her, also got under way and steamed after us. Seeing that the enemy carried a gun and was manning it, we opened fire without further formality.

The first salvo fell four hundred yards wide—my gunnery officer was still on board the *Tirranna*—but the second straddled the target and at the third a red flash showed that we had scored a hit. The enemy crew abandoned their gun and we promptly ceased fire; but then the enemy's gun was once more trained on us and our guns roared again. It was enough. After the fourth salvo we could cease fire. Almost at the same moment the enemy disappeared into a rain squall and we stormed after her. Visibility had dropped to two hundred yards and for ten minutes we searched in vain—then the curtain of rain lifted suddenly to reveal her hove-to and offering no further resistance. The two ships lay close to each other for minutes on end before we could make any further move, as our boarding party had to wait for their motorboat to catch up with the ship. When at length they boarded the enemy they found that she was the 6,731-ton Norwegian *Talley- rand,* Captain Foyn master, owned by the Wilhelmsen Line, registered in Oslo, and built at a Kiel shipyard in 1927. Out of five ships we had captured, this was the third that had been built in Germany.

The *Talleyrand* was bound from Fremantle to Capetown, where she was due to refuel and proceed to England. Her cargo consisted of wool, wheat, steel bars and teak. She had been fitted with a gun and degaussed in Sydney; this was her first voyage as an armed ship. There were only about four hundred tons of fuel in her tanks—too little to get her home without replenishing. She carried a crew of thirty-six Norwegians, including one woman, but had suffered no casualties. Her external appearance was rather unusual. Her hull was black, her name was clearly painted at bow and stern;

her upper works and masts were gray, "so that she should not look like a British ship," said her master. He added that he had planned to break through to Norway instead of going to England, and this was later confirmed by his crew. He told us of the difficulty of raising a crew in Australia, as men from neutral ships did not want to join any ship bound for England. He personally had had no difficulty, as his crew were privy to his intentions.

Captain Foyn had heard in Australia of the disappearance of the *Tirranna* and *City of Baghdad*. He said that the Australians assumed that the *Tirranna* had absconded to Italian Somaliland or Madagascar; the German raider was believed to be on the equator. When Foyn stepped on board *Atlantis* he was greeted joyfully by his colleague from the *Tirranna*.

"Well, Gundersen," cried Foyn, slapping him on the back, "are you still afraid of crossing the Indian Ocean? That's what you said in Melbourne."

"Did I say that?"

"You did indeed—that's what I heard."

Captain Gundersen was silent for a moment—then he looked Foyn straight in the eye and they both roared with laughter.

"It seems," gasped Foyn, "that the Wilhelmsen Company's skippers enjoy the favors of the same ladies in Melbourne."

From these and other exchanges I could see that the Tonsberg firm of Wilhelmsen must be very much a family concern. The meeting of the two ships' companies reunited friends and relations including two brothers who had not seen each other for years and even a father and son—the one a coxswain, the other a shipwright.

I hesitated for some time before deciding whether to send the *Talleyrand* home as a prize; she was undamaged apart from a hole in the bows, and she was carrying a valuable cargo. My final decision was largely influenced by the fact that to detail a prize crew for her from my ship's company would weaken our fighting capacity. Even more important was the fact that she had only four hundred tons of oil left and to replenish her from *Atlantis* would leave our stocks dangerously low. It was the fuel factor that finally decided the *Talleyrand*'s fate. Before sinking her we took her further south to a position where we could strip her of everything useful without fear of interruption. Her stores added two whole months to our endurance.

The transfer began with the removal of the Norwegian crew with all their effects to the *Tirranna*, which also took over her boats; *Atlantis* appropriated only one motorboat which appeared particularly sound and seaworthy. In addition to his own personal effects, each man of her crew took his bedding and mess gear; the rest of the crockery, together with the fresh fruit and food stores, went to *Atlantis*, which also pumped four hundred and twenty tons of oil out of the *Talleyrand* into her own tanks in five hours. At the last moment Captain Foyn had a word with Lieutenant Fehler, as a result of which a number of cases of whiskey were transferred from the *Talleyrand* to the *Tirranna*. At least Captain Foyn and his friends would not run dry during their long homeward voyage.

Early in the afternoon operations were completed and the *Talleyrand* was ready to be sunk. First of all, however, our aircraft took off in an attempt to shoot down the ship's aerial and drop bombs on her. Neither experiment was successful. The pilot had better luck in shooting up the bridge and radio cabin with his machine guns; and the pattern of his hits showed that it might be possible to compel a ship to stop by machine-gun fire from the air before she could send out a distress signal. When the seaplane returned, Fehler and his demolition party boarded the *Talleyrand* to lay scuttling charges; this time they took 160 lbs. of explosives with them. The first charge went off at 5:46 P.M., followed closely by a second and then by a heavy explosion in the engine room. The whole ship shuddered and began to sink by the stern; within eight minutes she had disappeared beneath the waves.

The *Talleyrand* was the fourth ship we had sunk, bringing our total to 28,205 tons; our fifth victim was now ready to sail for home.

I was just writing up my log when Sub-Lieutenant

(S) Waldmann—the *Tirranna*'s prize captain—came to take his leave. He showed some anxiety about fuel supplies as his chief engineer was sure that there were no more than five hundred and fifty-six tons in the bunkers. I sent my own chief engineer over to make a personal inspection and he reported that the *Tirranna* was carrying at least six hundred and sixty-three tons— sufficient to steam for several days at seventeen knots if necessary, or to run at nine knots for forty days. Besides this there were a further one hundred and fifty tons—enough for several days steaming and more than a merchant ship usually carries in reserve. Waldmann did not seem convinced by this report but he made no further comment when I proposed that he should sail at five minutes past midnight.

I told him to make for St. Nazaire or, in an emergency, Lorient or Bayonne. I had carefully worked out a course that would take him outside British or German submarine patrol areas, and I warned him to pay particular attention to Italian U-boats which had recently been active off the Azores. I wrote in his orders that he was to keep well away from the Cape and to steer midway between Bahia and Freetown, where enemy carriers might be operating; thence between the Cape Verde Islands and the Azores to the Spanish coast. The final danger area—Cape Finisterre—must be traversed at high speed at night and using zigzags during the day. Any encounters with other ships were to be avoided and his gun was to be left undisguised; he could use it in self-defense and he was to do all in his power to prevent the ship from falling into enemy hands. I warned him to guard against any attempt by the prisoners—including the Norwegians—to put the scuttling charges out of action or to signal to other ships; any such attempts were to be prevented by armed force and saboteurs were to be shot. He was to make this clear to the prisoners.

I was careful to impress two other points on him —he was not to let himself be influenced by enemy radio propaganda, and on arrival he was to make himself personally responsible for keeping the prisoners isolated, especially the women. If any petty local official should attempt to disregard this order, the prisoners were to be kept on board pending a decision by the Naval Staff; the prize crew was not to be disbanded until the matter of the prisoners had been settled. Furthermore, mail from the *Atlantis* was under no circumstances to be handed over to anyone but the Admiralty courier; if necessary Waldmann was to deliver the mail in Berlin with his own hands.

At 00:05 on Monday, August 5, 1940, the two ships sounded their sirens in farewell and our prize disappeared in the darkness, carrying with her eighteen of my men as crew, ninety-five white prisoners including six women and three children, and one hundred and seventy-nine Asiatics—a total of two hundred and ninety-two souls. To assist Waldmann in the smooth running of the ship, I gave him the services of the former first mate of the *Goldenfels,* Sub-Lieutenant (S) Mund.

"I have the fullest confidence," I wrote in my log, "that these two officers will successfully complete the mission assigned to them." Nor was my confidence to be misplaced.

There was an unwonted quiet on board *Atlantis,* with no prisoners strolling about or playing chess or cards, nor any children's voices ringing across the decks; we missed the calm politeness of the Asiatics and the chanting of the Lascars as they worked. It took several days to complete repairs. My chief engineer reported that it had been high time to renew the cylinders, as some of them were leaking and others had carbonized exhaust ports or very dirty pistons; the starboard engine was ready and repairs to the port engine would, he said, be completed in five days. It was no use being impatient. While the ship was being converted at Bremen I had repeatedly asked for the engines to be overhauled but each time I had been assured that this was quite unnecessary as a major overhaul had been carried out in the summer of 1939.

On August 8 the Naval Staff wirelessed: *"Your short signal of July 14 received after being repeated by* Pinguin *and relayed by U-boat UA. You are to be congratulated on your successes. It is assumed that your report of sinkings does not include mined ships."* The same afternoon our W/T office picked up a signal sent *en clair* from Mauritius and repeated in merchant navy code which augured well for the future. According to this, any ship which heard a distress signal being jammed was to signal its own position at once and if possible to give a bearing of the SOS and the jamming transmission. Ships were advised that it was far better to send a hundred unnecessary reports rather than to leave a single SOS unanswered.

If this directive were adhered to, it would enable us to get a clear picture of British ships' positions. We could also send out our own calls and jam them, to make the enemy give away their own whereabouts. By sending out false distress signals and position reports we could create such chaos that the enemy would confuse genuine calls with fake ones.

On August 11 our repairs were completed. In trials on the 12th *Atlantis* reached seventeen knots, with engines running smoothly. Thereafter we cruised for days on end along the routes that had been followed by the *Tirranna* and the *City of Baghdad,* but we saw nothing and heard only the wireless signals of distant ships and occasionally an SOS, which betokened that our rivals—the other raiders—were not idle.

10

FIVE MONTHS AT SEA

Until August 26 we cruised between Mauritius and Rodriguez, covering the old *Tirranna* route and the shipping lanes between the Sunda Strait, Singapore, Durban and Colombo. The weather was very squally at times and we often lay with engines stopped, drifting and waiting. The night of the 25th was dark and cloudy but the lookout on the starboard wing of the bridge suddenly sighted something darker than the sky. "Silhouette bearing green one-oh!" he shouted. The officer of the watch followed his pointing finger, then quickly sounded the alarm. A fully darkened ship was approaching.

We spent the next few minutes slowly maneuvering into position astern of the enemy. We lost her once in a rainstorm, raced after her at fourteen knots, found her again and then hung in her wake; we noticed that after steaming at five or six knots she suddenly dropped down to one knot—a very suspicious way for an ordinary merchant ship to behave at night and in wartime. She was still too far off for us to make her out clearly and my lookouts' estimates of her varied from an aircraft carrier to a destroyer; only my chief coxswain agreed with me that she was an ordinary merchant ship of 4,000-6,000 tons, but even we were not certain as she had an unusually long flat deck. It seemed unlikely that she had sighted us until we turned toward her; the ordinary English binoculars would not be powerful enough to pick us up—we knew this from tests we had made with captured glasses. Even Zeiss night glasses with sevenfold magnification only showed her up as a shadow.

Could she be a decoy? It seemed improbable; there were so few raiders at sea and the enemy could not be sure that there was one in the Indian Ocean. The last D/F bearing taken on *Atlantis* was five weeks old and incomplete at that. Nor was she likely to be a ship with engine trouble, as we had just completed a search all along the Mauritius route and must have seen her. The longer we looked at her the more certain we became that she was not a warship on patrol, so there remained only one solution—she must be an auxiliary cruiser. This assumption was given added weight by her unusual behavior, especially when soon after 5 A.M. she turned slowly away to port. I deliberated for a long time whether to steam away before first light or to send a boarding party over to capture and scuttle her. The latter course would expose my crew to great danger, since we must assume that the ship was indeed an auxiliary cruiser and that she had already sighted *Atlantis*. Realizing that it was now too late to move out of sight before dawn, I decided to bear down suddenly at high speed and smother the ship with gunfire at close range.

Sunrise was at 6:45; first light half an hour earlier. We had to maneuver so that by 5:30 the enemy would be outlined against the eastern sky; but at 5:30 the enemy turned slowly to port and thus came on to a course almost parallel with our own. She was now barely moving through the water. For a few minutes it looked as though she was going to turn toward us and attack, but she suddenly ceased to turn and seemed to have stopped altogether. We still could not identify her precisely but she appeared to have the lines of a conventional freighter. The possibility of her being the *Pinguin* faded—in any case that ship had no right to be there—because her forecastle was too high and her poop too low; the lightening sky revealed a small stern and other peculiarly English characteristics. I hesitated for a moment longer. Would an auxiliary cruiser allow herself to get into such an unfavorable tactical position? Would it not be sufficient to order this ship to stop in the usual way? But she had behaved in far too suspicious a manner during the night; I decided to take no risks and make a surprise attack.

At 5:50 A.M. we increased speed to eight knots; within six minutes the range was down to 3,000 yards. At this point I fired a torpedo. It missed and I ordered the guns to open fire. The range was now down to 2,400 yards and in our first salvo three out of four shells scored hits; flames shot up amidships and on the bridge, spreading swiftly to the whole ship and lighting up the gun on her poop and her red-painted funnel. Her crew ran, panicstricken, to swing out their boats; but as they had not manned their gun we did not fire again. It was obvious by now that she was not an auxiliary cruiser but a perfectly ordinary merchant ship— the only question was why she had maneuvered in such a suspect manner. We steamed up to within 300 yards of her—so close that we could see her original gray paint showing in places through the wartime coat of black; her funnel had a black boot-topping and she had two lifeboats amidships, a dinghy aft, a 4.7 inch gun and five hatches. We launched our motorboats to pick up the survivors. The heavy seas made this difficult and I dismissed the boarding party; because of the flames they could only have boarded the ship from the windward side and here the waves were leaping ten and twelve feet up the ship's side. Our boats moved first toward the men who were clinging on to pieces of wreckage, the red lamps on their lifejackets dancing on the waves like fairy lights. The ship was burning like a haystack and even before we had finished picking up her survivors, her bridge structure collapsed with a crash and a shower of sparks.

Navy Luger

I waited impatiently for the survivors to be brought on board. We had attacked the ship in the middle of a shipping lane; she was burning so brightly that she was probably visible for fifty miles or more and would have to be sunk as soon as possible. When the boats eventually came alongside we hoisted the wounded carefully up on deck, leaving the uninjured to struggle as

best they could up the swaying jacob's ladder. If a man
jumped for the ladder too soon he risked having his
legs crushed by the upward surge of the boat against
the ship's side. At less than three hundred yards we
opened fire again on the now abandoned ship, causing
splinters to fly as far as *Atlantis* herself. Our shells tore
great holes in her sides, through which poured streams
of coal, and in ten minutes the ship had capsized. For
a moment her hull lay upon the sea like a huge whale,
then the waves engulfed her and five of her men as
well.

The ship was the *King City* of 4,744 tons, belonging to the Reardon Smith Line of Cardiff, built in
England in 1928. The five men lost included four
young cadets trapped in their cabin beneath the blazing
bridge, and a cabin boy. Besides the master the survivors consisted of twenty-six English and twelve colored seamen—Arabs from Aden or half-castes from
Goa. Two of the Englishmen were badly wounded and
had to be operated on immediately, but one of them
was beyond all human aid and died on the operating
table.

Interrogation of her master revealed that the *King
City* was on charter to the Admiralty with 7,136 tons
of Welsh coal and 201 tons of coke from Cardiff,
bound for Singapore. Her engines were in such a bad
state that she could not maintain her planned speed of
nine knots. Since meeting the trade winds she had only
made good 4½ knots and that very morning she had
stopped altogether when the boiler-room ventilation
failed. She had only sighted us three minutes before we
attacked. The three hits had set fire to the bridge and
the crews' quarters and wounded the second mate as
he lay in his bunk; the master had been asleep and was
awakened by the news that a strange ship was approaching. He said he had heard it casually rumored in
Durban that a raider was believed to be in the Indian
Ocean, but he had not heard any details of her presumed position nor been told to take any special precautions.

Early next morning the dead English seaman was
committed to the sea beneath his country's flag in the

presence of myself and a party of my men. Like the *Talleyrand,* the *King City* had not been able to use her wireless, which meant that we could remain in the area without fear of discovery. All the same, we made certain alterations to *Atlantis*'s appearance in the course of the next few days, including the removal of some of her derricks, which were kept in reserve in the event of an accurate description of the ship being circulated.

I was by now getting very worried about the *Tirranna.* I had provided her captain with three ready-coded signals for despatch in *Atlantis*'s name at three widely separated points, but so far we had not picked up any of them. I could not believe that she had been lost and yet we would certainly have intercepted any transmission from her. While I was trying to work this out we intercepted an SOS from the English tanker *British Commander* on the 600-meter wavelength: *"QQQ—stopped by unknown vessel in position . . ."* and then, *"vessel now shelling us."* Both signals were promptly repeated by Natal and the ether began to crackle. Walvis Bay, Algoa Bay and Takoradi followed suit, while Lourenço Marques indiscreetly relayed news to a Portuguese ship and then repeated both SOS signals. Natal called the *British Commander* but got no answer; then Natal, Mombasa and Mauritius alternately sent out warnings and tried to call up the tanker. There was uproar everywhere.

Here was proof that the *Pinguin* had arrived in the Indian Ocean—not at all conveniently for us; although she would provide us with an alibi for a few days, it would limit our stay in Mauritian waters and was bound to put enemy shipping more on the alert. On the other hand it would now be possible for one raider to help the other by sending out fake distress signals and position reports, to confuse the enemy patrols—a typical example of the vital role played by wireless in ocean warfare.

Wireless was in any case playing an increasingly important part in our activities. If the *Tirranna* did not make a signal between August 28 and 31 we would have to try with our own much less powerful transmitter to warn the Naval Staff of her impending arrival in waters patrolled by Axis U-boats.

There was great excitement on board on the day that the Naval Staff signaled the latest batch of rewards. Fifty Second Class Iron Crosses were awarded to the ship, while I myself received the First Class. I now had eighty Iron Crosses at my disposal and after much deliberation with my officers, I found it possible to make a fair distribution of them among the ship's company, not forgetting those who had played no small part in fitting out the ship and devising her camouflage.

On September 1, 1940—the anniversary of the outbreak of war—I mustered the crew and conferred the decorations on those who had been selected to receive them. On this day also we recorded our fifth month at sea, having covered a total distance of 27,435 miles since leaving Germany. Our total of 473 men on board included eighty-two white and sixty-two Asiatic prisoners.

11

THE *BENARTY* 'S MAILS

We had still heard nothing from the *Tirranna*. The time had come to try once again to send a signal with our own transmitter. So we steamed southward for two days at eleven knots and then transmitted at short intervals on 18 and 24 meters a brief message: *"Prize No. 1 sailed August 4."*

One hour later came Berlin's acknowledgment: *"Prize No. 1 sailed September 4."*

I swore aloud. Now I would have to signal all over again and give the enemy another opportunity of getting a bearing on my position—all because some fool in Germany was too sleepy to pay attention. But if I did not correct Berlin's error, the *Tirranna* would arrive unheralded in the Bay of Biscay—and that must not happen at any price. Once more we steamed for a whole day at eleven knots—this time to the east—before making a signal on 24 meters: *"7,230-ton ship Tirranna ETA St. Nazaire about September 10, carries gun aft, deck cargo of lorries. Atlantis."* This time the message got through and the following day the Naval Staff signaled congratulations.

Meanwhile we had turned north again to search along the *Tirranna's* route as far as Mauritius. The weather was perfect, with visibility up to forty miles in the dry air and an even temperature of 68°.

One forenoon a lookout sighted a yellow funnel fourteen miles off in the morning haze and we raced to action stations. As *Atlantis* swung around I could see that the ship was a tanker, for her funnel was well aft. We increased to fourteen knots and the range began to drop rapidly; soon we could make out a small gun on the enemy's stern. An opportune rain squall drifted between the ships and I took advantage of this to come even closer to our victim. When the rain cleared the range was down to 8,500 yards and we could see that the other ship's suspicions had been aroused; her gun was being manned and trained on us as she turned sharply onto a course parallel with ours. But we held on our course as though we had seen nothing and after seven minutes the tanker altered sharply to pass astern of us and regain her original course. Her gunners left their gun and it was clear that the suspicions of the tanker's skipper were so far set at rest that he had not bothered to signal a report on "the approach of a suspicious-looking vessel." He was either completely deceived by *Atlantis's* disguise, even at so short a range, or else he was waiting for the routine time for sending SOS signals.

The three vital minutes crawled by but no signal came from the tanker. Then she hoisted the British ensign for a short time, but *Atlantis* took no notice. We were waiting until the SOS time was past. Suddenly we opened fire at no more than 6,800 yards range. The first salvo fell short but the second straddled the target. My W/T office reported at once that the ship was sending out SOS with all urgency and did not even stop when hit by shells. Our own radio was of course jamming hers.

Two minutes after opening fire, *Atlantis* suddenly veered to starboard. "What's happening?" I called.

"Helm jammed to starboard," came the report, followed closely by "enemy has stopped transmitting."

"Cease fire!" I ordered, but immediately there came, "Enemy is manning his gun! Enemy is returning fire!"

Three times the tanker's gun fired, her shells churning up white columns of water astern of us while her SOS signals continued to shriek through the ether. After a delay that seemed endless, *Atlantis* began to answer her rudder again—she was being controlled from the after steering position—and swung back on to her course; and our guns roared again until at last another hit silenced both the enemy's gun and her wireless. The tanker stopped and hoisted the international flag signal W—*"I require medical assistance."*

"DR," I answered, *"I am coming to your aid,"* and steamed close up while the boarding party got ready.

All of a sudden the W/T office reported, "Enemy is transmitting again!" and without hesitation we opened fire with every gun that would bear. At such short range the results were devastating. Flames shot up from the tanker and in a few seconds her bridge and stern were blazing. We had to stop that SOS signal from going out at all costs, even if it meant the loss of valuable diesel oil for our engines. We ceased fire and I sent away the boarding party. A few minutes later they signaled, *"Engine room burning. Oil in the bilges has caught fire. Flames have reached bridge. Oil leaking from safety valves of cargo fuel tanks. Risk of major explosion."* The tanker's fate was sealed. The boarding party returned with thirty-seven Englishmen in two boats—three of them seriously wounded. There had been no Asiatics aboard.

I learned that the burning tanker was the *Athelking* of 9,557 tons, owned by the United Molasses Co.

of Liverpool, and built in Newcastle in 1926. Three members of her crew were missing including Captain Tomkins, her master, who had been killed by a direct hit as he was leaving the ship.

"Why did you send QQQ," I asked, "after asking me for medical assistance?"

"We didn't," answered the two radio operators, "Captain Tomkins may have done it. He was still on the bridge near the radio room after we had left."

I could not help pointing out that he might have still been alive if he had not sent that SOS.

We hoisted the tanker's boats inboard and carefully reduced them to matchwood, in order to leave no trace. Then we opened fire again; our shells tore great holes in the tanker's side and thirty-seven minutes later she sank by the stern. Barely three and a half hours had gone by since we had first sighted her.

There was now no point in keeping *Atlantis* on course for Madagascar as it was fair to assume that the enemy would be patrolling the focal points of all routes south of that island. There would be better chances of success near the Sunda Strait and I accordingly shaped course to the northeast. Strangely enough the *Athelking*'s SOS had not been acknowledged by any shore station. Our W/T office had only picked up an urgent call to Mauritius from "VKYI"—an unknown vessel —which was not answered. Six minutes later the same ship had called Natal, also in vain, and finally had addressed to "GBXZ"—all British warships—a message of thirty-six code groups which she did not wait to hear acknowledged. There was no way of ascertaining whether this signal had had any connection with the *Athelking* and it suddenly occurred to me that perhaps the "QQQ" message we had heard after the tankers had hoisted flag "W" had been made by some other ship repeating the *Athelking*'s signal—in which case our second attack on the tanker had been unnecessary. Since the *Athelking*'s master was dead we would never know the truth.

The very next day we sighted another ship—this time on the port quarter—and I turned *Atlantis* toward her before the alarm bells had stopped sounding. I sent for Lieutenant Bulla, the seaplane pilot, and told him to take off and try to carry away the enemy's aerial.

"The most important thing is to prevent the enemy from using his wireless," I said. "The surest and least harmful method would be to tear down his aerial and if that does not work, to shoot up his radio cabin. Do you think you can do it?"

"I can try, sir," he replied. "I can certainly do it with my machine guns."

He saluted and disappeared. His plane was loaded with 60 gallons of petrol, two 110-lb. bombs and 120 rounds of 2 cm ammunition, as well as a grapnel on a line. Then I had a brainwave. I had learned from our colored prisoners how little they liked loud noises and how quickly they would panic at the sound of gunfire. I sent a messenger to summon Bulla back to the bridge.

"Listen, I have had an idea. We will try to launch your plane under cover of a rain squall. You must then try to pull down the enemy's aerial, but above all you must shoot up the funnel and bridge with your guns. That will distract the attention of the bridge watch from us and—with any luck—will cause the Asiatic stokers to panic and leave their posts. By riddling the funnel you will reduce the draught from the boilers. That alone may suffice to stop the ship. While you are attacking I will bring *Atlantis* up at full speed. Is that clear?"

"Aye, aye, sir." Bulla saluted again and hurried away.

A rough estimate, taken in the eye of the sun against a glittering sea, put the range at about eighteen miles; all we could see of the enemy were her masts and lofty funnels.

"Probably an English ship," said my officer of the watch, "anyway, the bearing is constant. We are on converging courses."

Just half an hour later we saw the enemy turn away to the north; it was obvious that she had sighted us. We also turned away, but to the south; the enemy altered course again and finally moved out of sight in a northeasterly direction. Her master was clearly a cautious individual who was keeping to the letter of the Admiralty's orders; it would be of no use to try our usual tactics of overhauling him slowly. As we turned back again to follow, a light haze on the horizon hid the ship from view; when she came in sight again she was back on her original course, so we moved away again as though trying to shake her off.

Just at the right moment as luck would have it a curtain of rain came between us, enabling us to turn to port and launch the seaplane. The wind had eased but there was a short, choppy sea, forerunner of a distant storm. Our hearts were in our mouths as the fragile machine danced on the waves like a drunken butterfly, its propeller revolving slowly as the pilot wrestled to bring the plane into the wind in the lee of *Atlantis*. Then the engine roared into life, a wake creamed behind her and she was off. As soon as she was well into the air we turned and increased speed to follow the enemy.

The latter promptly radioed "QQQ" and gave her position but—much to our delight—with an error in dead reckoning of about sixty miles. The aircraft's attack with bombs and machine guns so distracted the crew that they never noticed our approach. After twenty-two minutes Bulla made a last run-in, wirelessed the target's course and speed and landed safely alongside us. But we had no time to spare for the plane; the enemy had disappeared into a rain squall five miles away and it took us seven long minutes to find her again. When we did, it was to see the ship still on her old course, with no one visible on deck or at the gun. We hoisted our ensign and flag signal to heave-to, unmasking our forward guns. Nothing happened. The after guns were also unmasked—but still nothing happened. We fired two rounds from the forward guns ahead of the ship at 3,400 yards and, when the enemy still showed no sign of life, a salvo right over her. I was loath to set her on fire as I hoped to take her undamaged and perhaps capture some secret papers of recent date. At last—after ten minutes—the enemy ship lost way and stopped and our boarding party started over toward her; but while they were still on the way, she began to signal "QQQ" again adding, "*S.S.* Benarty *bombed by plane from ship.*"

"Put a shot into her bridge, Kasch!" I ordered. The shell, fired from less than a mile away, burst in No. 3 hold immediately abaft the bridge, hurling the hatch cover high in the air and setting fire to the cargo. I signaled to the boarding party to extinguish the fire if possible. The British crew were running for the boats, and the commander of the boarding party's first action was to pick the ship's master, chief engineer and chief steward out of their boat and bring them back on board their own ship. They were ready enough to cooperate once they saw that the battle had gone against them, and the chief engineer himself attended to the safety valves in the engine room. The telegraphs on the bridge and in the engine room still stood at "Full speed ahead," which showed that the engines had been abandoned before the ship was stopped. My guess about the stokers had been right.

Assisted by an extra working party, the boarding party made a thorough search of the ship, looking for secret documents, fresh food and clothing for the British crew. They found that although she was old and slow, the *Benarty* was carrying important mail for the British Admiralty. This was the most valuable haul that we had made so far and Mohr took away whole sackfuls of documents, even down to the contents of the wastepaper baskets. Of the crew, consisting of twenty-two undoubted "beachcombers" and twenty-seven Chinese, three were slightly wounded but nobody had been killed. The ship was still burning merrily and the fire was put out with difficulty.

The *Benarty* was a 5,800-tonner built in Glasgow in 1926, belonging to the Ben Line, W. Thomsen & Co. of Leith, bound from Rangoon to Avonmouth and Liverpool with a cargo—according to her master —of nothing but rice and oil cakes. But this was soon proved to be a barefaced lie; in fact the ship was carrying wolfram, zinc concentrate, paraffin, hides, beans and tea as well as thirty bags of mail—making a total of almost incalculable value. As soon as all her secret papers, fresh food and mails had been trans-

ferred, we fired scuttling charges in three places and the
Bernarty sank quickly by the stern. We kept two of her
bigger boats and a small "skimmer" and smashed the
rest into small pieces.

A glance at the chart showed that a line drawn between the positions where the *Athelking* and *Benarty*
had sent out their SOS signals led directly to the Sunda
Strait; it seemed wiser to steer south instead of continuing east, and to wait until the excitement had died
down.

As we began to sort out the documents we had
seized, the practice of collecting the contents of all
wastepaper baskets in captured ships proved its value
once again. Since the day we had found the merchant
navy code and a number of reciphering tables on board
the *City of Baghdad* we had been able to read all the
enemy's merchant ship W/T traffic, until the reciphering tables were changed. Now, with the aid of some
messages retrieved from the wastepaper basket in the
Benarty's wireless cabin, my radio officer was able to
achieve a partial decryption of the cipher, which was
completed for him by our Naval Staff in Berlin. The
latter correctly assumed from his queries that *Atlantis*
was now in possession of some code books, and subsequently sent us from time to time the interpretation of
various newly deciphered groups, so that henceforward
we were able to read the current enemy cipher traffic
quite regularly. Unfortunately for us, some prisoners
put ashore on an island by another raider had noticed
that their captors could read the navy code, and as a
result the enemy soon began to restrict W/T traffic and
to change the tables more frequently.

The *Benarty*'s log showed that after sailing in convoy from England to Sierra Leone she had proceeded
independently to Durban; thence she had steered a
course between Réunion and Madagascar for Aden
and from there via the Maldive Islands to Rangoon. On
her return voyage she had followed a route more to the
south and east. Her master told us that he had heard
in Rangoon that the *Kemmendine* was overdue and
that only one of her boats had been found. He had
not been warned about German raiders but the route

given him—from 6°30′N, 95°E through two other positions to 30°S, 48°E—took him in an unusually wide sweep to the south. The covering letter to his sailing orders stressed the importance of guarding against careless talk on shore. The log revealed further that the master had had to use force to prevent his Chinese hands from leaving the ship at Rangoon. On the day before she was sunk, the *Benarty* had picked up the *Athelking*'s SOS, and this had naturally aroused misgivings. The most interesting fact to emerge from these papers was that at least three routes intersected at position 22°S, 68°E—close to where the *Tirranna* had been captured. Over the next two days we carefully scrutinized all the official mail from the British authorities in India, including a bag of secret correspondence for the India Office in which were some British secret service reports; among these last was a report on Mr. Hilton, the husband of Mrs. Hilton, recently a passenger in the *Kemmendine*.

On September 12 I cleared the lower deck and gave the crew a talk on what we had learned from the captured papers. For instance, it was clear from the latest Admiralty directives that merchant navy skippers had been put on their guard; they were quicker to take evasive action and were not deterred from sending an SOS even when shelled by a raider. On the morning of the day she was sunk the *Benarty* had received a coded signal from the Admiralty which caused her to post extra lookouts; the misgivings evoked by the approach of *Atlantis* had only been allayed when the latter had maintained her course as the *Benarty* turned away. This, I explained, showed how important it was for us to keep up our guise of innocence for as long as possible. We had also discovered that enemy skippers never expected us to disguise our ship as British; they expected to find us flying neutral colors, and one of our prisoners had taken us for a Greek ship. I told my men that we would see if we could look even more like a British ship by removing the camouflage from our after gun. The appearance of an unarmed British ship in these waters would deceive nobody, but it might be possible to make our 15 cm gun look like a British 4. 7inch. We also discovered that the SOS signals we had picked up in both the last engagements had been made by ships other than our immediate target; I resolved to be more careful in future in my appraisal of reports from the W/T office about enemy transmissions, otherwise we could not hope to capture a ship without setting her on fire. We wanted to seize ships intact, not only because they were valuable as prizes but because they could provide accommodation for our prisoners.

I wrote in my log at this time: "I am very surprised that the British should use a ship like the *Benarty* for carrying secret mails; the loss of this ship will soon become known when the mail does not arrive, at any rate in Burma. Our prisoners are convinced, by the way, that we are getting information about shipping movements from Fifth Column agents, which enables us to lie in ambush for our victims. This belief was strengthened when we steamed at fifteen knots from 12:30 to 6:00 P.M. on September 8 and then captured the *Athelking* on the 9th."

12

THE LOSS OF THE *TIRRANNA*

The dull, rainy weather and the monotony of shipboard routine was beginning to have a bad effect on the crew's morale. They showed little enthusiasm even when Berlin relayed a report in the *Daily Express* that the *Tirranna* was long overdue at Mombasa. How long ago it seemed since we had captured the *Tirranna* —she must be almost home by now.

An event now occurred which I had been awaiting with no little trepidation—the *Pinguin's* operational area began to overlap with ours. She signaled that she was in position 33°S, 68°E, which in my view was much too close to us for safety; I was all the more perturbed when it became clear that she had not adhered to the carefully planned dividing line between our two areas. However since the *Pinguin* was apparently operating outside her own area with the Naval Staff's approval, I decided that in future I would not be so meticulous in keeping to mine.

Another long weary period of waiting followed. The Chinese prisoners were released from the quarantine in which they had been confined by Dr. Reil after one of them had died from unknown causes. We put them to work about the ship like their Arabian and Indian fellow prisoners and soon every department had its quota of colored assistants—Arabs in the engine room, Indians for deck work, colored stewards in the petty officers' quarters; I took on "Boy Mohammed," a grand old Indian with a white beard, and on "curry days" our rice was cooked by Indians and served by Chinese.

From noon on September 18—a full week since the sinking of the *Benarty*—we began to cruise at nine knots in a south-southeasterly direction toward the Australian route, taking care not to reach it too soon lest chance should bring us in contact—and perhaps in conflict—with the *Pinguin*. I was fully prepared to see several days pass before we found a ship, but I preferred to carry out a search all the same, rather than remain inactive, particularly since the Battle of Britain was now being contested so bitterly in Europe.

On the evening of September 19 I stopped engines to conserve fuel and we drifted in the heavy swell. At 10:55 P.M. the port bridge lookout sighted a vessel almost on our quarter, emitting heavy smoke; she was the fourth ship to announce her presence in this way. She seemed to be steering a westerly course— presumably outward bound from Australia. I sounded the alarm and rang down for full speed ahead, as we would soon be plainly visible to the enemy in the moonlight. But a flare of sparks from the funnel forced me to reduce speed again until the engines had warmed up; the most we could do without throwing out sparks was twelve knots.

The enemy looked like a fairly large ship with several funnels and she was steaming at high speed without lights. After consulting with Kasch, I decided to circle around and come up astern of her to attack, allowing myself until midnight to do so. Eight minutes after midnight we altered sharply toward the target, which was now bearing 045 degrees, and opened our flaps to accustom the gunners' eyes to the darkness. The tension grew as the range dropped to 5,000 yards and we still could not identify the target. A few minutes later the range was down to 3,500 yards but we did not appear to have been sighted. Then I realized that she was a passenger ship and decided to try to stop her by signal and capture her intact, so that I could transfer our prisoners to her.

We challenged her with our signal lamp and immediately got the reply, *"Understood."*

"Don't use your wireless," I signaled and again the enemy replied, *"Understood."*

Then I sent, *"Heave-to or I fire,"* and this was duly acknowledged. *"What ship?"* I asked and the answer came "Commissaire Ramel."

I told her to await my boat and she stopped, blew off steam and switched on her lights. At the same time our searchlight illuminated her in a blinding glare, revealing a black-hulled passenger ship with yellow upper works like a P & O liner; she had a small gun—as yet not manned—on her poop. After exchanging signals we resumed our approach at ten knots, but then our W/T office reported just what I had been hoping to avoid. "Enemy is transmitting."

I hesitated for a moment before opening fire, for after all she was a passenger ship, but it could not be avoided and seconds later our shells crashed into her at almost point-blank range, while we jammed her transmissions on the 600-meter wavelength. Her radio went dead and we promptly ceased fire, but her bridge and forecastle were already in flames. Then her radio started up again on 18 meters, *"RRRR—position . . .* Commissaire Ramel *gunned."* Meanwhile her first SOS had been picked up and relayed by Mauritius and other shore stations. With this second transmission there was no point in holding back any longer; some fifty 6 inch high-explosive shells with tracer were poured into her. We saw fires starting inside and through her port holes. Soon a sheet of flame spread like lightning over the whole ship. Outlined against the glare, two boats dropped into the water—then a signal was flashed over and over again, *"Send a boat. Send a boat."* By the time we had launched our boat—no easy matter in such a seaway—and it had reached the ship, the flames had spread so far that no one could get on board her. One boat lay off her stern while two others were drifting about in the darkness, making no attempt to reach us; one of them had stepped a mast and was clearly about to hoist sail.

Our motorboat had never been designed for such a task. She was an open boat with no buoyancy tanks and her canvas hood could not be used without unsighting the coxswain, yet somehow she won through, rounding up the boats like any sheepdog. Forty-two Englishmen, fourteen white and seven black French citizens, including one slightly wounded man, were at length assembled on our decks; one Englishman and two negroes had been killed by shellfire. The three boats were cast adrift as soon as the survivors' few possessions had been saved. The ship was burning very brightly so we opened fire with our after gun to finish her off, and she went under in an inferno of steam and flame. The reflection of the fire on the clouds 2,000 feet above us vanished and in the oppressive darkness that followed a damp breeze blew in our faces, piping a faint but mournful tune.

We learned that our latest victim was a 10,061-ton ship carrying a cargo of grease, hides, soap, fruit and jam from Australia to England. Her master, Captain Mackenzie, was a 64-year-old Scot who had lived in retirement for many years in Sidney; but when the British requisitioned the *Commissaire Ramel* in Suva, they took him away from his golf clubs and sent him to sail the ship on her first voyage to England. A crew had been assembled with the greatest difficulty—most of them seemed to have been picked straight off the beaches—because the original French crew had deserted. Her French skipper, M. Sabouret, was traveling in her as a passenger.

When the British master was brought to my cabin I could not contain my anger and gave him a harsh dressing down for his perfidy in sending an SOS after heaving-to. He took my rebuke calmly and with dignity and at length the truth came out. The French first mate was on watch when we attacked and it was he who had taken it upon himself to heave-to and blow off steam. As soon as they realized that something was wrong, Mackenzie and Sabouret, who were playing bridge in the saloon, dashed together on to the bridge; as Mackenzie passed the wireless cabin he shouted, "Send an SOS!" before he knew all that had happened. He was not really to blame for this and I at once apologized for the hard words I had thrown at his head.

The survivors told us later that the cargo had been so badly stowed that even in calm weather the ship rolled worse than any of the crew had ever experienced. She had sailed from Fremantle on September 12 and was due to refuel at Capetown. None of her officers had heard anything about a raider operating in these waters, although they knew about the loss of the *Tirranna* and *Talleyrand*.

We steamed away at fifteen knots, heading a little north of due east; I had chosen this course because the British Admiral in Colombo would now have on his chart five positions from which "QQQ" and "RRR" signals had been made. If he joined these positions together he would assume that the raider was either on a southeasterly or southwesterly course, according to the position in which the *Pinguin* had recently captured a ship called the *Lahore*. Attractive as the proposition seemed, I must at all costs keep away from the Australian track and disappear as quickly as I could into some remote area, to keep the enemy in the dark about my movements. For the same reason I did not dare to send a signal reporting my position. It would have been very convenient if the *Pinguin* had reported capturing another ship at this juncture, as it would have completely covered my tracks. I regretted that we had not been given direct instructions by the Naval Staff to rendezvous somewhere, as at one point we were only eighty miles apart and a conference would have been very helpful to both of us.

In the long intervals of waiting I made some of my officers give lectures—Mohr, for instance, spoke on his analysis of the *Benarty*'s mails—and we carried out some slight alterations to the camouflage. These captured papers gave us a wonderful insight into the economic position of Burma, alterations in shipping movements, the position in Indo-China and methods of delivering arms to China via the Burma Road.

But on September 27 fate dealt us our first real blow.

First the Naval Staff reported that, while on passage, the *Tirranna* had sighted eight ships including a cruiser; had passed between Madeira and the Azores; had not received the Naval Staff's orders but had nonetheless completed the voyage according to plan. We assumed that she had safely reached port and great jubilation reigned on board. We looked upon the *Tirranna* as a gift from us to our countrymen at war and as a proof of the value of our long sojourn at sea, cut off from all the pleasures of life on shore.

Then, a few hours later, came the second part of the signal. Having got the impression from enemy broadcasts that St. Nazaire was mined, the prize captain had anchored off Cap Ferret and had sent Sub-Lieutenant Mund on shore to telephone from Arcachon. The 17-knot ship had thereupon been ordered to steam to Bordeaux at ten knots without zigzagging. The next day she had been torpedoed by a British submarine off the Gironde.

To say that the news of the *Tirranna*'s loss aroused our indignation would be grossly to underestimate our feelings—the whole ship's company was outraged, and so was I. Our wrath waxed greater as further details came through. The whole of the prize crew had been saved but sixty prisoners were missing. The prize captain, Sub-Lieutenant Waldmann, had been awarded the Iron Cross, Second Class, by the commander-in-chief, since he was in no way to blame for the loss of his ship. But—the question was on the lips of all of us—who *was* to blame and how could this have happened? Did the "people at the top" ever stop to think what it meant to a raider's crew to see their efforts so frustrated, merely because someone had blundered somewhere? Bad wireless communications were obviously at the bottom of it all—what other explanation could there be for the fact that the *Tirranna* had been using the wrong reception wave for seven whole weeks? Did not the coastal defense stations at Bordeaux know anything about the danger of submarines, or were their defenses so weak that they could not provide an air escort for the last twenty miles of the ship's voyage? Why had she not been ordered to zigzag? And above all, why in heaven's name did the Naval Staff think it unnecessary to tell us whether the secret documents had been saved and whether the passengers had been rescued?

I could not refrain from confiding rather bitterly to my log that the Naval Staff had never given us any information about other European ports to which prizes could be sent. I was kept completely in the dark as to the situation in Somaliland, Japan or Madagascar. The Naval Staff must know that very few ships carried enough fuel to get them to Europe, so where could they replenish en route? Could prisoners be landed in Somaliland and would prize ships be interned in Madagascar or Japan? Was it possible to send messages from Somililand through Madagascar? There was no end to these questions—but there was no answer to them. The *Tirranna* was gone. Neither my crew nor I ever quite got over her loss.

From then on we drifted for days on end, occasionally steaming back on our tracks. We sighted nothing, but we did not expect to sight anything. We were deliberately keeping clear of the shipping lanes; there would be time enough later to increase our score of sinkings.

And the score to date wasn't a bad record. In the first six months of her operations, *Atlantis* had covered 31,638 miles and sunk nine ships totaling 65,598 tons, excluding ships sunk on the mines she had laid off Agulhas. The number of prisoners on board had varied greatly, reaching its maximum of three hundred and sixty-five in August, just before the departure of the *Tirranna*. At the moment, we had two hundred and ninety-three survivors on board, including one hundred and ninety-seven white men, two half-caste Portuguese, fifty Indians, ten Arabs, twenty-seven Chinese and seven negroes. The lives of sixteen white men and five colored men had been lost in action.

In the course of our voyage we had so far made the following changes in the *Atlantis*'s disguise:

March 22—Second funnel and mine-sweeper rig removed.

March 23 to April 1—Disguised as Norwegian s.s. *Knute Nelson*.

April 1 to 27—Disguised as Russian auxiliary cruiser *Kim*.

April 27 to May 21—Disguised as Japanese s.s. *Kasii Maru*.

May 21 to June 18—Disguised as Dutch s.s. *Abbekerk*.

June 18 to today—Disguised as Norwegian s.s. *Tarifa*.

On October 1 I closed the entry in my log with the words, "As my next step I plan to make a sortie into the Sunda Strait."

13

THE EPIC OF THE *DURMITOR*

A few days later we reached our new ambush position in the Sunda Strait and began to cruise slowly across the shipping lanes, while the crew spent their time fishing for sharks or exercising at the guns. I was delighted to read a signal from the Naval Staff to "Ship 10" (*Thor*) promising to keep the raider better informed of political and military developments; not all the raiders were able to listen-in to the German State Broadcasting. Obviously the *Thor*'s captain felt the same way about the Naval Staff's so-called "news bulletins" as I did—and had said so. Any real news of the war was always welcome, whereas none of us had any use or information about the introduction of new peaks for part-time railwaymen's caps or the repetition of stale news from the front.

In an endeavor to find out the route taken by ships after leaving the Sunda Strait, I ordered the seaplane to be launched for a reconnaissance flight as soon as the sea was calm enough. She took off under difficulties as a defect in her engine made it essential not to drop below 1,800 r.p.m. On landing she broke an engine strut, not for the first time. But we had no spares left and it was doubtful whether we could repair the damage. Our range of vision was once more reduced to the horizon as seen from the masthead.

Just after sunrise on October 22 we sighted a ship. At first we thought that she was a Dutch passenger ship—her white upper works appeared only dimly in the silvery morning haze—but a few minutes later we were able to distinguish the national colors painted on her side as Yugoslav. I approached to within 3,000 yards and as usual hoisted the ensign and the flag signal to heave-to, but it was some time before the Yugoslavs realized that they had company. Eventually a figure clad in pyjamas clambered on to the bridge and acknowledged our signal. The Yugoslav stopped and so did we. She began to use her wireless so we unmasked our guns, whereupon she ceased to transmit.

While our boarding party was getting ready, she seized the opportunity of sending out two SOS messages, but it did not seem worthwhile to open fire on her as she did not give any indication of her position. *"What ship?"* she signaled by radio. *"this is the* Durmitor," and again, *"Who is calling me? Please answer. This is the* Durmitor." Finally she sent, *"S. S. Durmitor from Lourenço Marques for Japan via Batavia. Who are you?"* To put an end to these radioed questions I answered by light, "R—OK—EB—QRT." (Understood—wait—stop transmitting), whereupon the transmissions ceased and the ship signaled by flag that she had stopped her engines.

The boarding party reported that the *Durmitor* was a ship of 5,623 tons registered in Dubrovnik, carrying a cargo of 8,200 tons of salt from Torrevieja in Spain destined for Hiroshima and Miike in Japan. According to her charter her cargo was the property of the Bussan Company. The master said that his ship was due to call at Batavia as an intermediate port for further orders. I declared the *Durmitor* a prize in accordance with Article 39, section 3, and Article 40, section 1, of the Prize Regulations—"Assistance given to the enemy by wireless despite orders to remain silent"—and Articles 23, section 3 and 28, section 2— "Carrying contraband via enemy ports." Before loading salt at Torrevieja she had carried coal from Cardiff to Oran, whence she had sailed the day before the British had shelled the French fleet there. She had spent a week in Gibraltar and several more in Lourenço Marques because she could not fill her bunkers; coal from Natal was only being supplied by the British to their own and Japanese ships. Her long sojourn in port had resulted in her hull getting so badly fouled that she could not do more than seven knots. She carried a crew of thirty-seven men, fifteen tons of drinking water, twenty tons of washing water and food for eight or ten days. Her stock of 450–500 tons of coal was supposed to last her as far as Japan.

I decided to put my prisoners and official mail on board the *Durmitor* and send her to Italian Somaliland with a prize crew of twelve men under the command of Sub-Lieutenant (S) Dehnel. I ordered him to sail the *Durmitor* provisionally to a rendezvous point where she could wait until *Atlantis* had completed operations in the Sunda Strait and had assembled enough stores for the prisoners to take with them on their journey. I set the date of the rendezvous for October 26.

Then we began once again to search the intersection points off the Sunda Strait, always drifting or steaming at slow speed; but there was nothing to be seen except the monsoon-swept sea and the cloudy skies. The temperature was in the eighties and the air was sultry and humid. To be honest, the sultriness was not confined to the air. Stories were beginning to reach my ears from the lower deck of criticism of my plans, of dissatisfaction with the division of duties and of quarrels among the men. Remembering how often Nerger had had to suppress mutiny on board the *Wolf* by energetic measures, I was determined not to allow matters to reach such a pass in my ship. Most of the discontent was doubtless due to the heat and lack of sleep, which was affecting the men's nerves, together with disappointment that matters in Europe were moving so slowly. I decided to take the bull by the horns and on October 25 I cleared lower deck.

I told the men that I was well aware of their grumblings and then in a few words I sketched the general situation of the war, warning them that the end was by no means in sight. For that reason, I said, we must stay at sea for as long as possible, which was why I had had to reduce their rations. I explained that the present system of giving them less meat, fats and butter was in fact better for them in tropical weather than their previous diet.

"The more privileges I grant you," I said, "the more I do for you, the more you ask for. We have been at sea now for seven months. The time has come to speak plainly before it is too late, and I have to take more drastic steps. I know that the heat makes us all slack, but cooler weather, will bring cooler judgment. At all costs the discipline of the ship must be maintained, for our lives depend upon it."

I then offered them a measure of encouragement by describing plans I was completing to ease the strain. Four men in turn from each division would spend one week in sick bay "on leave," with no duties to perform except at action stations. Secondly I promised them "make and mend clothes" time on one afternoon a week—probably a Wednesday; thirdly, on really hot days, the situation permitting, work schedules would be restricted to between 8 and 11 A.M. and 3 and 5 P.M. I would also try to arrange to spend Christmas in some undisturbed area.

"But I will not tolerate any unconstructive criticism or grousing behind my back," I warned. "Such things don't help to improve matters, on the contrary they make life harder for everyone."

The men seemed to have understood me and, as I expected, their bad temper began to disappear. It faded completely next morning—Sunday October 26 —when we sighted a ship. It was in fact only the *Durmitor,* but there was little time for grumbling now, as every available man was kept fully occupied with the job of transferring the prisoners.

The advantages of having two hundred and sixty fewer mouths to feed on board *Atlantis* greatly outweighed the fact that the *Durmitor* was ill equipped to carry extra people. The conditions in which the prisoners would have to live were frankly bad; for they would have to be accommodated in the holds on top of the cargo of salt, without mattresses, blankets or hammocks. Only those over fifty years of age were allowed mattresses. The strain on our bakery was such that we could only give the *Durmitor* a week's supply of bread, while drinking water was available only in small quantities and there was no water at all for washing. I explained these conditions to the prisoners in advance and expressly warned them that acts of sabotage or mutiny would be ruthlessly suppressed. Then I sent for all the merchant skippers and, after telling them the same thing, I asked them to give their word of honor not to attempt any disobedience against the prize captain's authority nor to engage in sabotage or mutiny. All the skippers gave me their word and subsequently kept it.

The food on board the *Durmitor* was shared equally by all ranks including the Yugoslav crew whose morale, according to Dehnel, was very low as they had had no news from their families for months. The ship was in very poor shape; only one boiler was watertight, all the others were leaking and her top speed was only seven knots. She was crawling with cockroaches, bugs and rats.

We remained hove-to until Dehnel and his little party had limped out of sight. None of us could have guessed at that time what adventures were in store for that young officer and his ancient command before they reached the Somaliland coast.

Things first began to go wrong when they discovered a hollow space beneath the coal, which meant that they had not got enough to reach port. Undismayed, Dehnel hoisted sail, using the hatch-cover tarpaulins to help the monsoon drive his 5,000-ton ship along. To maintain steam he gradually broke up everything that would burn—barrels, hatch covers, lagging, derricks, doors, furniture, wooden paneling—everything was hacked to pieces or sawn up with the only handsaw on board. He made briquettes out of a mixture of coaldust, ashes, paint, sawdust, asphalt, petroleum and grease. There was nothing he did not use as fuel.

When he noticed signs of mutiny among the prisoners he quietened them by pointing to a convenient smoke cloud on the horizon and hinting that *Atlantis* was within call and would descend upon them at a word from him. The older skippers helped to restore order and the prisoners grew calmer when Dehnel openly showed them what supplies were left and explained how every economy must be enforced. After many dan-

gers and difficulties he eventually reached the Somaliland coast—not Mogadiscio, which had recently been
shelled by the Royal Navy, but the small port of Chisimaio, where for lack of proper charts he ran the ship
aground. However he got her off again and brought her
in on November 23, 1940. All he had left on board
were 440 lbs. of coal, 650 lbs. of beans and not a drop
of water. On landing he was promptly arrested together
with his crew and his own prisoners and driven trium-
phantly through the countryside in lorries before he
could clear up the mistake and obtain his freedom.

That, in brief, was the epic of Sub-Lieutenant
Dehnel and the *Durmitor*. Four months later he and
his prize crew were to rejoin *Atlantis* from the *Tannenfels*.

14

TANKERS AND TOP SECRETS

On the night of November 8, when we were a
day's run north of the Equator, we sighted an eastbound ship and steamed cautiously after her. It was
impossible at first to make out any details but she
seemed to have an unusually long flat deck like a
tanker—or a cruiser? She was standing out against
the lighter part of the sky while *Atlantis* had as her
background a darker horizon and heavy rain clouds.
After twenty minutes we were near enough to identify
the ship as a badly blacked-out tanker.

I gave the order to open flaps but as yet I with-
held the order to fire. At five hundred yards our searchlight blazed out and shone blindingly on the target;
we saw at once that the ship's gun was not manned and
also that she had a black funnel with a large red K.

We called her up by lamp, signaling, *"Heave-to at once. Do not use your wireless. What ship?"*

The answer was, *"Teddy, Oslo. What do you want?"*

"You will be searched," I replied.

The tanker signaled, "OK."

"Do not use your radio. It is forbidden," I repeated.

There was a pause and the tanker asked, *"May we proceed?"*

"No, wait for my boat."

"Who are you?" asked the tanker and was given the answer, *"HMS* Antenor."

The tanker then blew three long blasts on her siren to show that she had stopped; her gun was still under its cover. My boarding party rushed to get ready. I had chosen the name of the British auxiliary cruiser *Antenor* because she looked rather like the *Atlantis* and I hoped to keep up the deception until the search party had got on board and could prevent the ship from sending out an SOS. The tanker's crew made no attempt to lower a ladder; they were blinded by the glare of the searchlight and it was not until my men were already on board that the Norwegians realized who they were. And by then it was too late.

The *Teddy,* a 6,748-ton ship, was carrying 10,000 tons of fuel oil from Abadan to Singapore. I placed a prize crew under Sub-Lieutenant Breuers aboard her and told him to take her to a rendezvous some five hundred miles to the south. Her Norwegian master, Captain Torlutken, said that he had five hundred tons of diesel oil in his bunkers, but I left it until later before deciding whether *Atlantis* should take this over for herself or whether the prize should be sailed to Japan; visibility at the moment was too bad to start transferring oil and I did not want to risk being surprised. The moon had set and with frequent rain squalls making the night still darker, it became difficult to maneuver the two ships. Then our first cutter had a mishap, getting a cable around its propeller so that it had to be towed in by another launch; and when that had been accomplished the second launch lost its rudder while on the way to take the rest of the Norwegians off their ship. An attempt to steer with ropes was not successful and in the end we had to launch yet another boat to take the orders to the prize crew and to bring in the first one.

The captured tanker was sailed to position "Mangrove," slightly south of the equator, where we were due to meet her again after making a sortie into the Gulf of Bengal. I had also decided that we would take over her diesel oil and 1,000 tons of fuel oil and then sink her. I had reached this decision when I realized that the *Teddy*'s five hundred tons of diesel fuel would increase *Atlantis*'s endurance by another two months. The need to be self-supporting was of paramount importance, more important than holding the *Teddy* in reserve for the oil-fuel-burning *Orion*. I should add that my decision was largely influenced by the complete lack of any comprehensive Naval Staff directive or prearranged code groups concerning the capture of tankers, or of adequate foresight in planning mutual support between diesel-engined and oil-burning raiders.

Almost at the same time the *Pinguin* had captured a tanker off Australia that was carrying 10,000 tons of diesel oil. As there was no special groups for signaling about tankers, the *Pinguin* merely reported that her bunkers were topped up. Had she signaled, *"I have 10,000 tons of diesel oil available,"* I would have known that she had more than enough fuel for *Atlantis* and it would not have been necessary to sink the *Teddy;* she could have been either despatched as an oiler for the *Orion* or sent to Japan.

Within twenty-four hours we had achieved our next success. After taking off in calm weather, the seaplane returned to report sighting an eastbound ship to the north. I at once shaped course to bring *Atlantis* up with her after dark. We worked up to full speed and as night fell with the usual suddenness of the tropics, the enemy appeared exactly as scheduled. At the same time the moon rose and by its light we could plainly recognize the ship—she was another large tanker. But the moon's rays illuminated *Atlantis* just as brightly and as we closed her, the tanker suddenly turned away and radioed feverishly, *"QQQ—QQQ— QQQ—Position* 2°34′N 70° 56′E Ole Jacob *unknown ship has turned now coming after us."* The *Ole Jacob* was another Norwegian tanker. I was determined not to lose her at any price. I realized that if I ordered the guns to fire now, the target would be in flames in a matter of seconds and her cargo—which might be just what was wanted for *Atlantis*'s engines—would be lost. We would have to try to board the tanker and subdue her by force. But before trying this rather desperate expedient, the ship—like the *Teddy*—must be deceived and reassured by an exchange of signals; so I signaled by light that we were HMS *Antenor.*

"Please stop following me," came from the tanker. We called her up several times until she replied, *"Norwegian tanker."*

"Please stop. I wish to search you," we signaled.

"Understood."

"HMS Antenor *here."*

"Ole Jacob—*OK*—stopped."

But although the tanker did heave-to she also repeated her "QQQ" signal on 600 meters, adding, *"Stopped by unknown ship."*

We steamed up astern of the *Ole Jacob* with our motorboat hanging ready at the davits; my adjutant and Kamenz, the navigating officer, were already in it, with ten men of the boarding party hidden under a tarpaulin. Mohr had slipped a British uniform jacket over his German one to keep up the deception as long as possible. The boat was slipped and crept toward the tanker. The Norwegians could only see the two officers and the coxswain, but not the men under the tarpaulin who were armed to the teeth with pistols cocked and hand grenades in their belts.

The water was calm except for a long swell coming up from the south, in which boat and tanker rolled together. As the boat came nearer our officers could see a row of heads at the tanker's rail, looking suspiciously down at them. An arc-lamp shone out, lighting up the tanker's gun and the men standing behind it in their low-crowned steel helmets. The gun was trained menacingly on *Atlantis*.

Success hung upon a thread. As the light shone down upon him, Mohr dazzled the Norwegians with his own flashlight. The boat bumped alongside the tanker's lofty hull. A group of men were waiting amidships —presumably the ship's officers. Rifle barrels glittered in the lamplight—they were clearly determined not to allow anyone on board. Someone shouted, "Are you British?" Mohr called back something unintelligible in English which was drowned by the crunching of the boat against the hull. The light was still shining down into the boat but there was nothing to be seen; the tarpaulin gave no hint of the men beneath it and the Norwegians were still dazzled by Mohr's light. The boat was rising and falling on the swell like a lift, one moment dropping below the tanker's waterline and on the next rising level with the guardrail.

"Take your jacket off!" hissed Kamenz to Mohr. The next time the boat lifted. Mohr whispered, "Go!" and seizing hold of the rail he and his companion swung themselves on to the deck, pistols between their teeth. Before the Norwegians knew what had happened, their rifles were wrenched out of their hands and flung overboard. "Hands up!" yelled Mohr and Kamenz, "go on! Hands up!" Turning to the waiting boat they shouted, "Board her!" Quick as a flash the tarpaulin was flung back and the ten men scattered swiftly over the decks, while the two officers raced over the network of pipes toward the bridge. As they ran they smelt the heavy odor of petrol vapor that enveloped the whole ship and through their minds ran the thought, "If anything goes wrong now, we're in for a fiery trip to Heaven."

The Norwegians evidently had the same idea. The master, who was standing on the bridge companion, surrendered as soon as he saw what had happened and ordered the gunners to stay away from their gun. A minute later Mohr signaled to me, *"Tanker* Ole Jacob *with 10,000 tons of aviation spirit. Am cancelling her QQQ message."* He did this with the tanker's own transmitter. Among the ships which had picked up these signals was the British Blue Funnel liner *Automedon,* which we were to meet later.

The 8,306-ton *Ole Jacob,* registered at Arendal, was on her way from Singapore to Suez. Naturally such a valuable ship could not be sunk. I placed Kamenz in command of her and sent her off to position "Rattang," three hundred miles south of the equator, close to where the *Teddy* was lying. We brought the tanker's master, Captain Leif Krogh, and most of his thirty-three man crew on board *Atlantis,* leaving only a few of them to assist in running the *Ole Jacob.* During the next few hours Colombo radio repeatedly called the *Ole Jacob;* the A/S trawler which had picked up her original SOS and its cancellation joined in and repeated both signals. The *Ole Jacob* herself of course refrained from making any further signals. Now that the area was alerted and our exact position had been reported, I decided to get away with all speed; we left the tanker at dusk and steamed southward at fifteen knots.

A signal received that night from the Naval Staff said that the alarm caused by the appearance of German raiders had led to their being reported even in the Bay of Bengal, "although," said Berlin, "there are none there." I could not help smiling, for the Naval Staff naturally had no idea that I was in the Bay—such a move was not in my operational orders.

Our next victim came in sight the very next morning, showing up in the clear light as a thin smoke cloud on the southwestern horizon. The sea was as smooth as glass. We stopped for a while to get a better idea of her course and speed and then began a careful approach. The range was more than eighteen miles. Neither we nor the enemy—which we could now identify as a Blue Funnel liner—made the slightest alteration of course and since we were converging, the range dropped rapidly. When it was down to 4,600 yards *Atlantis* turned sharply to starboard, cleared for action, and hoisted the usual signals, at the same time firing a warning shot over the ship.

The enemy promptly started to wireless for help,

so we opened fire in earnest. The range was now down to 2,000 yards and the very first shots took effect, causing heavy damage amidships and on the bridge. The ship got as far as signaling *"RRR Automedon 41 . . ."* when our jamming set drowned her transmission. Her master and everyone on the bridge were killed by the first salvo; with the next three salvoes we scored eleven hits amidships and then ceased fire. A man appeared near the ship's gun and we sent over three more salvoes, scoring hits fore and aft.

Eventually the *Automedon* came to a stop—she had ceased to transmit after her aerial had been shot away—and our boarding party set off. When they got on board they were confronted by a terrible spectacle. Our shells had riddled the upper works, smashed the davits and boats to pieces, holed the funnel and made the bridge almost inaccessible. The captain's cabin and that of the first officer were a heap of splintered wreckage; dead and wounded, many of them hideously mangled, lay groaning in pools of blood on the deck. The body of the master lay upon the bridge where he had been killed by a direct hit. Another officer, killed by a splinter, lay in front of the charthouse with half his face blown away. A third was missing altogether and was probably lying underneath the wreckage of the first officer's cabin—the latter was also wounded. The shipwright had been killed outright and out of six badly wounded men, the chief steward and boatswain died of their injuries on board *Atlantis*.

As the bills of lading had been destroyed, it was not until we had opened up the hatches that we learned that the ship had been carrying general cargo from Liverpool via Durban for Penang, Singapore, Hong Kong and Shanghai. But what general cargo! There were thousands of crates containing airplanes, motor cars, uniforms, caps, machinery spares, bicycles, cigarettes, microscopes, steel, copper sheet, umbrellas, cameras, sewing machines, sanitary equipment, medicine, whiskey, beer, food—and mail. A cargo worth millions. Since the *Automedon* had been stopped in what was obviously a busy thoroughfare, I gave orders that only the most important portions of her cargo were to be salved—such as could be transferred in a matter of hours. This included all the food and frozen meat and one hundred and twenty mailbags, besides the crew's personal effects. There were thirty-seven Englishmen on board, three passengers including one woman, and fifty-six colored men, mostly Chinese; among the latter were some members of the crew of the *Anglo Saxon,* which had been sunk in the Atlantic while on the way to Hong Kong.

Several times I had to extend the time limit that I had set for emptying the ship of stores. Lieutenant Fehler, commanding the search party, had a remarkable talent for locating something of value a few minutes before he was due to return. *"Have discovered 550 cases of whiskey in No. 3 hold,"* he semaphored, *"request permission to delay return."* And half an hour later he signaled, *"Have just discovered 2½ million Chesterfield cigarettes. Request permission delay return."* We were well into the afternoon before I finally ordered clearance operations to cease. I had had to abandon any idea of towing the *Automedon* to some lonely spot, there to search her at our leisure, as her steering gear had been wrecked. As in the case of the other ships, the English cooperated willingly with us; they soon realized that it was in their own interest to transfer as much food as possible and they appreciated the—to them—unexpected care with which we had salvaged their personal possessions. But in their haste they forgot to tell us that there were 6,000 gallons of cider in a special cold room. They only remembered it when the *Automedon* had been scuttled and sunk; whereupon there were mutual lamentations among victors and vanquished.

An examination of the captured documents showed that we had made a specially good haul this time. The death of the ship's master and of so many of her officers had prevented the destruction of her secret papers which, by the irony of fate, had survived the holocaust. All the Admiralty instructions, the sailing orders, and the secret logs fell into our hands, and after forcing the steel safe in the master's cabin we found the Merchant Navy Code and Nos. 7, 8 and 9 reciphering tables. Nor was that all. In the mail room next to the master's cabin, Mohr had found a large quantity of secret mail marked "Safe Hand. British Master Only." The contents of this exceeded all our expectations; there was all the correspondence at the highest security level for British commander-in-chief, Far East, new cipher tables for the fleet, notices to mariners, information on minefields and swept channels, maps and charts, British secret service reports and finally a secret appreciation by the war cabinet which gave a comprehensive review of the defense plans for the Far East, directives for the defense of Singapore and the disposition of the enemy's land, sea and air forces. The substance and quality of this information was so outstanding that when the Japanese saw them later they thought at first the papers were forged. They could not believe in so much good luck.

When the *Automedon* sank by the stern at 3:07 P.M. on November 11, 1940, *Atlantis* had sunk thirteen ships totaling 93,803 tons and carrying seventeen guns. During the night the W/T office picked up a coded signal from the *Helenus*, a sister ship of the *Automedon*, and shortly afterward Colombo was heard calling the ship; both were alarmed by receiving the incomplete SOS signal from her. Then the *Helenus* signaled to Colombo, "Automedon *2008 GMT 11 November 'RRR* Automedon *lat. 04.-16.N. . . .'*" Bearings taken on this transmission showed that the *Helenus* was fairly near *Atlantis* on a parallel course, but for some extraordinary reason I was not informed of this fact until the following morning, by which time we had been on a different course for some hours and were too far away to overhaul the *Helenus*. The same evening Singapore radio called the *Durmitor* on 600 and 36 meters, asking her to reply on 36 meters—which she would have found rather difficult, even if she had been in a position to transmit, as she had no shortwave transmitter.

Early in the morning of November 13 we made contact with the *Teddy* and proceeded to clear everything useful out of her before sinking her with scuttling charges. The demolition party failed in their first attempt but there was nothing wrong with the next lot of explosives and the tanker blew up with a roar that, as somebody said at the time, must have sounded like the explosion of Krakatoa. The following day we were rejoined by the *Ole Jacob* and took over all the oil she could spare, leaving her only enough to reach a Japanese port. I had decided to send her to Japan for two reasons. Her cargo would be very valuable as a medium of exchange when negotiating for raider stores with the Japanese, but it was even more important to send to Berlin the documents we had taken from the *Automedon*. Their contents were such that, in my judgment, their delivery into German hands might have an important effect upon the conduct of the war as a whole. As there might be some difficulty in getting them through to Berlin, I decided to send them by the hand of my most experienced officer, Kamenz; and I accordingly placed him in command of the *Ole Jacob*. The tanker sailed on November 16 with a German prize crew and the crew of the *Teddy* as well as her own former company; she arrived in Kobe on December 6, where she refueled and sailed again to transfer her cargo to a Japanese tanker at Lamotrek in the Caroline Islands. Although the Japanese were delighted to acquire this high octane spirit for their planes, they were equally anxious to avoid being suspected of any breach of neutrality and had accordingly proposed to effect the transfer at a neutral place.

Admiral Wenneker, our naval attaché at Tokyo, secured 11,000 tons of diesel oil and an airplane in exchange for the aviation spirit; this represented one-third of all the oil made available to German raiders through the Japanese branch of our supply organization. The *Ole Jacob* did not return to Japan. After operating for some time as a supply ship to the raider *Orion,* she reached Bordeaux on July 19, 1941. Disguised as a high government official, Captain Kamenz reached Berlin via Siberia and Moscow; after making a personal report to the Naval Staff he was brought by U-boat to a supply ship in mid-Atlantic, whence he rejoined us in April, 1941.

Eventually we received news of the *Durmitor*'s safe arrival in Chisimaio, which gave us all something fresh to talk about; and on December 1 we heard that the *Pinguin* was about to sail a prize ship, the tanker *Storstadt*, home to Europe with four hundred prisoners and 10,000 tons of diesel oil from Borneo. Here at last was a chance of replenishing our supplies of fuel to the last cubic foot and I decided that it was worth risking a signal. I sent to the Naval Staff, *"Please send tanker to grid-square 'Tulip'*—Atlantis." The reply came immediately. The Naval Staff was proposing to use the *Storstadt* to refuel not only the *Atlantis* but the *Komet* and *Orion* as well. We were ordered to rendezvous with the *Pinguin* and on Sunday December 8 her captain, Krüder, came on board—the first German outside my own ship's company to set foot on our decks after three hundred days at sea. There was a tremendous reunion between our crews and despite the amount of work that remained to be done, celebrations were the order of the day. The *Storstadt* arrived the same evening and we began to refuel from her.

Next morning I returned the visit of the *Pinguin*'s captain. Just before I regained my own ship, a signal was received that read, *"To Atlantis. Commanding officer has been awarded the Knight's Cross of the Iron Cross. I offer captain and crew my warmest congratulations on this recognition of the outstanding success achieved by the ship. Commander-in-Chief,"*

PART THREE
AROUND THE WORLD
January–November 1941

15

THE KERGUELEN ISLANDS

That was our last operation west of Sumatra. I was getting worried about our supplies of drinking water and the engines were badly in need of overhaul; in any case, I had promised the crew that we would have a few days of rest and relaxation over Christmas. So for some time I had been considering a plan to steam to one of the uninhabited islands in the far south.

After carefully studying the sailing directions and having several long talks with one of the captured skippers, I decided that the Kerguelen Islands would be best suited to our needs; none of the other islands had any bays on their eastern side where a ship at anchor would be sheltered from the prevailing westerly gales. The Kerguelens are in latitude 50° south, in an area where no merchant ship normally goes; from the size and number of bays and inlets along the coast of the main island, it seemed almost certain that we should find a good anchorage where we could replenish our drinking water from glacier streams. Added to this was the fact that, although the Kerguelens are uninhabited, they had been well charted by several scientific expeditions over the years.

The *Pinguin* sailed off at noon on December 9. On leaving Captain Krüder signaled, *"Pleasant voyage and many thanks for everything. You have been our best prize to date."* I made a suitable reply and we got on with the job of transferring our prisoners to the *Storstadt* and taking oil out of her. Only three badly wounded Englishmen were retained on board *Atlantis*, as we could not arrange separate accommodations for them aboard the tanker and the latter would not be able to look after them as well as we could. We gave the *Storstadt* sixteen tons of water and food for sixty days as our share of the prisoners' rations and when the prize captain complained that he had only useless invalids to man his ship, we sent over two of our own ratings. We then sailed away, after ordering the *Storstadt* to remain at the rendezvous in case we or the *Pinguin* should capture a ship better equipped to accommodate the prisoners. As soon as we were out of sight, we turned and steamed steadily southward.

On Wednesday, December 11, I ordered "Sunday routine" and awarded the Iron Crosses that had been conferred by signal four days earlier. On December 1 it had been so hot that competitors in an open-air chess tournament were wearing only sun helmets and shorts; the trade wind which usually cooled the air had died away and the bridge lookouts were gasping in the pitiless heat; we were steaming through a perfect calm and the sea was like a mirror. By contrast, only a few days later the temperature had dropped to 60 degrees; men on watch at night put on their warmest clothing and even then they shivered, particularly on December 13 when in four hours the temperature dropped from 55 to 37 degrees. It began to blow strongly from the west, bringing rain and heavy seas—typical "Roaring Forties" weather.

In the crew's recreation space hung a blackboard on which Mohr used to write up any news interest. Now he pinned up a sheet of paper on which he had copied down all the information he had been able to extract from the Sailing Directions about the Kerguelen Islands.

"The Kerguelens are situated approximately 50° south and 70° east, and are about seventy miles in length and the same in breadth. They were discovered on February 12, 1772 by a Frenchman, Count Yves Josephe de Kerguelen-Trémerac, commanding the frigate *Fortune*. Thinking that he was off Australia, he did not trouble to land but returned instead hotfoot to France. A year later he again appeared off the islands as the leader of an expedition consisting of the *Gros Ventre* and *Oiseau*. He arrived on December 14, 1773, but did not land on this occasion either; only one boat from the *Oiseau* managed to gain the shore. On his return to France, the count was forced to confess his error. He was thrown into the Bastille and from there christened the island he had discovered 'The Land of Affliction.'

"The next man to land was Captain Cook, during his third voyage around the world. Between 1776 and 1873 the island was frequented by whale hunters and seal catchers. Few men have ventured far into the interior as the terrain is heavily ravined and so marshy that a man can sink up to his knees. The climate is harsh. There are no trees and therefore no timber; there is nothing for humans to eat, and food and fuel have to be imported. It is so difficult to move about that as much time is needed to walk ten miles as to cover thirty miles on normal going.

"In 1893 the French government farmed out the island to a Monsieur Bossière, who tried in vain to rear sheep there. Bossière says, "The interior consists of naked rocks and is dotted with marshland and lakes devoid of all wildlife. The lakes feed many vast waterfalls, one of them over 1,800 feet high. The highest mountain is Mount Ross, 5,600 feet, from which giant glaciers run east and west down to the sea. There are plenty of wild ducks, penguins and other seabirds to be found, and numerous rabbits. The only other animals are rats and mice, which abound.' "

All hands studied these details carefully. The Kerguelens did not seem to be exactly a Garden of Eden, but this was no time to be fussy. We hoped that the waterfalls—the real reason for our visit—would be close to the sea; we did not relish the thought of humping several hundreds of tons of water on board by the bucketful.

We raised the Kerguelens on December 14. In a heavy sea but exceptionally good visibility we saw a wild and forbidding coastline, topped by a range of snow-clad hills and with long narrow promontories flanked by scores of little islands and flat reefs. It was the first land we had seen for many a day. I sent away a reconnaissance party, well equipped with arms and signaling gear and disguised as whalers in leathers and furs, in the captured Norwegian motor cutter to survey Port Couvreux, an abandoned settlement used as winter headquarters by French settlers years before.

The party, consisting of the chief coxswain and seven men, was commanded by Mohr. At first there seemed to be nothing living among the gray rocks and drab hinterland. Then the coxswain pointed straight ahead and whispered, "Sir, I think I see someone standing on the beach." They all took a tighter grip on their rifles and pistols and ran the boat in at full speed. Mohr kept a careful watch all around. Four or five huts built of brownish timber stood in a small gully. They stood out clearly from their surroundings and appeared to be deserted. No smoke came from their chimneys but the sunlight was reflected from their windows. There were a couple of sheds close to the beach, near a small landing stage. It looked decayed. But what was that dark figure waddling clumsily about the beach, as though drunk? Why should a drunken man be walking about a beach on Kerguelen Island? While they were still gazing tensely across, the signalman, who had the keenest sight, suddenly laughed aloud. "That's Roland, sir!" Mohr turned to him non-plussed. "I am a Berliner, sir. The sea elephant in the Berlin Zoo is known as Roland." They ran the boat in to the beach as quickly as they could, keeping a sharp lookout, but apart from Roland there was not a living thing in sight. The landing stage creaked and groaned as they laid alongside it; planks splintered beneath their feet and dropped into the water. Eventually they got on to the beach. Roland waddled away and eyed them from a distance, then slid into the water.

It was strange to be standing on firm ground again amid a smell of blubber and earth. They stood there for a few minutes, sniffing the tang of the soil, before moving off to inspect the nearest shed. The door of one of them hung open on its hinges. On the beach they saw the skeleton of a boat eaten away by the passage of time. Beyond the beach, bare hills rose abruptly, with their tops almost in the clouds. Within three minutes they had reached the settlement. Amid a small group of buildings stood a larger house, not unlike a Swiss hotel, with a long glassed-in veranda in front. On entering, they found themselves in a fairly large living room furnished with a stove, a wooden table and two chairs, with a lamp hanging from the ceiling. A calendar on the wall bore the name of a colonial merchant in Tamatave, Madagascar, and was of the tear-off kind. It was illustrated with colored pictures of Madagascan girls with very little on, holding bottles of Pernod; the girls seemed to be out of place in that climate. The date on the calendar was November 18, 1936; so it was four years since anyone had visited the island.

In the next room, a battery of empty claret bottles showed that there really had been Frenchmen there. They found part of a loaf of bread which, astonishingly enough, had not gone mouldy; though hard, it was edible and even the mice had not nibbled it. Either the sailing directions were wrong about the "plague of mice" or else they had all died off. Then they came to the bedroom, where old-fashioned beds without blankets or pillows stood drearily against the walls, and everything smelt musty. They found some preserves and a box of dynamite with some tools in the workshop. Then they found a pigsty with two dead pigs in it. The remarkable climate had prevented them from putrefying. But why dead pigs? Why had Monsieur Bossière left his bread on the table and failed to eat his pork? It looked as though he had abandoned his house on the spur of the moment. Mohr suggested that what happened was probably that one day a ship had approached the island, possibly by mistake. It might have been the *Bougainville*—they found one of her sailors' cap ribbons on the floor—and Monsieur Bossière had rushed on board crying, "Take me with you. I never want to see this place again."

Mohr and his men reported to me over their portable radio that the island was quite clearly uninhabited.

The next task was to sound and buoy Gazelle Bay, the inner harbor of Foundry Branch, where *At-*

lantis had dropped her anchor for the first time after three hundred days at sea. I had chosen this spot because the *Antarctic Pilot* described it as the best of the natural harbors and because it would be easy to get our water supplies from neighboring streams. As soon as Gazelle Bay had been sounded and buoyed, *Atlantis* weighed and proceeded very slowly through a field of floating seaweed. After leaving the first two buoys to port, we were due to increase to half speed ahead and turn sharply to starboard. On weighing anchor we had switched on the echo sounder and this was recording six-and-a-half fathoms of water beneath us. Kühn and the boatswain were standing in the eyes of the ship; both anchors were ready to let go.

"Six-and-a-half," sang out the leadsman, "six-and-a-half . . . five fathoms . . . still five . . ."—"STOP BOTH!" Seconds later, with way still on her, *Atlantis* suddenly grounded on an uncharted reef which had not been located either by the sounding party or the echo sounder.

I tried to free the ship by putting both engines full astern, but she remained fast. I did not want to try any extreme measures until I knew how she lay. Soundings showed that the ship was resting on a small pinnacle of rock that rose steeply from a depth of ten fathoms, and was so narrow that it had escaped our sounding party. The damage control party reported that all oil bunkers and holds were intact. A diver went down to examine the hull and report on the ship's position and any damage sustained. His first report showed that the forepeak and No. 1 tank in the double bottom had been holed, but that the oil bunkers were fortunately untouched. The retractable minesweeping spar had been stove-in some five feet beyond its housed position and had penetrated some transverse bulkheads. The rent in the stem had caused the leak in No. 1 tank which contained eighty-two tons of drinking water; this gradually became tainted with sea water.

During the next thirty hours we made three attempts to get the ship off, but in vain. I tried not to think of what might happen if we were not successful —aground off an uninhabited and desolate coast, thousands of miles from the nearest civilization, in time of war. I climbed down into the flooded compartment with Kielhorn, a stoker and a telephonist; after pumping out the water with compressed air we made a careful survey of the damage from inside. We made our fourth attempt to get clear on December 16, after spending several sleepless nights in shifting everything movable to the after compartments. The ship was trimmed down 8½ degrees by the stern, but she still would not move. Next we laid the stern anchor out as far as possible and put both bower anchors down amidships. Heeling the ship over eight degrees, we shortened cable alternately on each side, while the engines were run full speed astern on a rising tide. The first attempt failed although we ran the engines for fifty-three minutes. At the second attempt the ship nearly swung into shallow water; she was held back only by her stern anchor, its hawser stretched almost to breaking point. The critical seconds went by, destroying our hope of getting the ship off on the flood tide.

With great difficulty we managed to shorten the wire hawser of the stern anchor and bring her stern more up into the wind before making our last effort. All hands were ordered on deck and then, on orders piped by the boatswain, they ran back and forth from starboard to port in an attempt to dislodge the ship by rolling her from side to side. Just as we were giving up hope, the ship shuddered and shook as though meeting heavy seas. Then she came upright and swung around until her stern was right into the wind.

Free again—at the last minute!

Preceded by a sounding party in a motorboat, we felt our way back into Foundry branch at dead slow speed. Very early next morning we launched a cutter and painstakingly buoyed the entrance all over again. At her second attempt, *Atlantis* entered Gazelle Bay without further mishap and dropped anchor with forty-five fathoms of cable in eight fathoms of water. The relief was unspeakable.

The secluded creek in which *Atlantis* now lay was walled in by three-hundred-foot cliffs; its entrance was barely six hundred feet wide. At the western side was a waterfall. From seaward the ship was almost hidden by the heights of the Jachmann peninsula. We began at once to overhaul engines and repair the hull.

While the ship was still fast on the reef, I had gone ashore with Mohr and Fehler to examine the possibility of getting supplies of water. If and when we found it, we would have to solve the problem of getting it on board; it was not a matter of a few pailfuls but of a thousand tons. As we ran through the entrance to Gazelle Bay we were overjoyed to see not only water but a real waterfall plunging conveniently down from the rocks above. One snag was immediately evident; because of shoaling water, the ship would only be able to get within one thousand yards of the waterfall. Had we got enough hose pipe on board to reach across that one-thousand yard gap? There was no way of knowing at that time. We hoped to use the waterfall as a sort of water tower; it was at much higher level than the ship under its own pressure. This sounded simple enough and our men were highly enthusiastic, as there is nothing sailors like more than working out a technical conundrum—the more complicated the better. Fehler, for instance, used to fling himself into such problems with astonishing vigor, usually starting his calculations on the assumption (being the demolitions officer) that something would have to be blown up.

As far as this waterfall was concerned, however, I strictly forbade any such thing and stressed that the matter must be approached more delicately. Fehler and Kielhorn then worked out a plan to insert a barrel into the waterfall to catch the flow, which would run through a hole in the barrel and thence through hose pipes to the ship. We viewed this scheme with some misgivings, but Fehler set to work to put it into effect with his usual zeal. Having found a suitable barrel, he cut a hole in it, secured guide ropes to it and brought it ashore. It was manhandled over the slippery volcanic rock to the waterfall, while another party of ratings followed with hose pipes. The ship was lying three hundred yards from the shore, while the waterfall was seven hundred yards inland. Our men clambered up with the heavy barrel until they were standing right next to the waterfall which was twenty-five feet wide, its waters feeding a small stream running into the bay. It was a herculean job to maneuver the barrel into position as the rush of water was immensely strong, but after three hours we succeeded and the barrel could at last be lowered to a position just clear of the waterfall, exactly as Fehler had planned. Whereupon Fehler went off on his favorite pastime of duckshooting.

Roland and his retinue, who had been interested spectators of these operations, moved a little way off when we began to haul the hose pipes across the beach. Dr. Sprung and Mohr went after them. All of a sudden the doctor jumped on to Roland's back. The great sea elephant grunted angrily and began to flap his way down to the water; he was too fat to dislodge his rider. So Dr. Sprung rode all the way down to the sea in this fashion while Mohr stood and filmed the whole thing. Roland's followers watched this remarkable episode in silent astonishment, but they suddenly took flight at the approach of my scotch terrier Ferry. The little dog was beside himself with delight to find land beneath his paws after being so long at sea. It was true that there were no trees on this island, but there were a lot of objects that could do duty as trees—wooden posts and moss-covered rocks. He was utterly happy; when he saw the doctor, whom he regarded as being in his charge, riding on a prehistoric mount, he rushed up to him yapping loudly and then dashed off toward a shining pebble which he suspected of having dared to move. Suddenly he began to yelp in a heart-rending way; we ran up and found him in a very nasty situation. He was spinning around like a top, barking furiously and snapping all around him at the huge seagulls which were hurling themselves down like Stukas at this unusual creature, their sharp beaks outstretched to seize him. We shooed the gulls away and took the terrified Ferry under our protection.

As dusk fell the first two hundred yards of hose pipe were in position from the waterfall to the beach. Early next morning we started work again and by midday the hose had reached the bay; by evening another length, buoyed up with lifebelts, was in position across the three hundred yards of water and the pipeline now stretched from the fall to the ship. We had exhausted our supplies of fuel pipe and fire hoses and some of the piping had to be made up out of sailcloth. At midnight the whole outcome of our two days' labor was imperiled by a violent squall which thundered down on *Atlantis* at nearly sixty miles an hour, snapping the hawsers that held the stern of the ship to the land, thus parting our hose pipes. But luckily the squall blew over as quickly as it had come and we were able to repair the damage.

Next morning Fehler was at the waterfall with his men. The moment had come when we would see if the voyage to Kerguelen Island and all our labors were in vain. I stood tensely on the quarterdeck by the end of the pipeline, waiting for the minute when the water would come aboard. Fehler and his men were hanging—almost literally—inside the waterfall. Personally I was still convinced that the water would carry the barrel away and Fehler with it. Then the barrel was swung into the fall and—miraculously—it stayed there. I saw the slack pipes stiffen, and then a stream of water as thick as my wrist spouted from the end on deck. This was more than we had dared hope for; the pressure was almost as great as that of the Blücher Bridge water point at Kiel. The water went on pouring into the *Atlantis* for two days and the whole plan was amazingly successful. My Chief Bos'un Russow, known throughout the Navy as "Franz," watched sadly as his beloved beer barrels were filled with glacier water instead of beer.

For several days I had been keeping an anxious eye on the slow progress made in repairing the hull. We were still not quite sure how far the damage extended or how the leaks could be stopped. The underwater oxy-acetylene burner kept on going out; and the one rating who knew how to work it had been shipped home in the *Tirranna*. So we had no alternative but to drill each damaged plate in turn, secure it with ropes and then hoist it laboriously up with the windlass. At the same time we had to pump out the forepeak and No. 1 tank and fill the holes with cement under pressure; four men took twelve hours to do this, working cramped together in the narrow pressure-filled compartment. The first results were satisfactory and the ship seemed to be water tight, but later there were signs of leaks elsewhere. Tired of getting incomplete reports, my chief engineer decided to go down himself and make a personal inspection, although he was not trained as a diver. What he told me confirmed my fears—the divers were unreliable and their reports contradictory. I decided to go down and see for myself. After a short lesson in the art of diving from a senior hand, I had myself lowered over the side. I found that the main source of leakage was where the double-bottom frames had been forced inward. The damage was indeed severe but not, thank heaven, irreparable.

Christmas Eve was upon us, yet up to now there had been no time for anyone to enjoy the period of rest and relaxation I had promised them. A strange feeling took hold of the men as the candles twinkled and the old German Christmas carols rang out. The Christmas trees, lovingly fashioned out of broomsticks, bits of string, wire and green paint, looked almost indistinguishable from the real thing. At divine service I read the story of the Nativity from the Gospel of St. Luke and then spoke of those at home whose thoughts would be with us at this time; as I did so, I suddenly realized what a strong bond of companionship had grown up among us. I distributed to each man a small parcel of good things taken from the Christmas mail we had found on board the *Automedon*. Outside a hurricane suddenly blew up and sent the anemometer off the dial; the wind screamed and howled, but *Atlantis* lay snugly protected in Gazelle Bay. On Christmas morning the upper deck was white with snow.

The commander-in-chief, Grand Admiral Raeder, did not forget to send us his greetings and added to them the award of fifteen Iron Crosses, Second Class, which I duly conferred at a Christmas Day parade on ratings who had distinguished themselves. On Boxing Day the first group of thirty-seven men went on shore leave. They were free to go wherever they chose and do as they pleased. They knew that the island was uninhabited but their comrades had told them that there was no lack of animal life and this they could now see for themselves. Penguins stood stiffly and proudly on the beach, each family a little apart from the next, or dived like arrows into the water. Comical gray seals suddenly sat up on the tough, tussocky grass, complaining angrily at being disturbed, while giant sea elephants lumbered about their equally imposing wives, belching thunderously. There were wild duck and ptarmigan, flocks of Cape pigeons, huge dark-brown seagulls and albatrosses; there were rabbits to be snared and shellfish to be collected. The shore-leave parties would return at the end of the day tired but happy, while the Bavarians among us who had not yet had their leave would yodel at the sight of the mountains, impatient to get ashore.

Day by day *Atlantis*'s outline was slowly changing. Her funnel was now wider, making the whole ship look smaller; and by removing the roof of the upper bridge we made the whole bridge structure look lower. After carrying out a thorough inspection from outside the ship, I was satisfied that the description given by the *Ole Jacob* survivors to the British authorities in Hong Kong would no longer apply to her; she really did look like the ship we had modeled her on—the Wilhelmsen Company's *Tamesis*. As she had only been built in 1939, the *Tamesis*'s external appearance was not universally known; her call sign was not even in Lloyd's Register of Shipping and I made a note to ask about this in my next signal to the Naval Staff.

We had had a tragic accident on Christmas Eve. While repainting the funnel a rating slipped and fell heavily to the deck, sustaining a fracture to both thighs. He died soon after one o'clock on the morning of December 29, and the news cast a shadow over the whole ship. Two days later he was buried with full military honors and we set a cross above what must surely be the southernmost of all German wargraves.

The wireless bulletins on New Year's Day told of

raider activity in the Indian Ocean, including the shelling of the phosphate station at Nauru—as we learned later by Admiral Eyssen in the *Komet*—and the setting ashore of four hundred and ninety prisoners on the island of Emaru by the same ship. Reports from Manila spoke of another raider that had been converted from the British freighter *Glengarry,* and from New Zealand came mention of my own name. The same day we got the first "bottle" of the year. The Naval Staff expressly banned any further operations such as the one against Nauru or the one planned against Rabaul—this was addressed to the *Komet;* "Naval Staff disapproves of the sinking of the tanker *Teddy* and the operations east of 80° east in November, of which Naval Staff was not kept informed"—that was meant for us.

Our days of rest and relaxation were coming to an end. The weather was very uncertain and the glass rose and fell sharply as winds of hurricane strength blew over our heads, but Gazelle Bay proved an ideal anchorage and the ship lay at her anchors without stirring. On January 10, 1941—twenty-six days after our arrival—we sailed again from Foundry Branch. At first we steered north at seven knots, later increasing to nine as we watched anxiously for signs of fresh leaks in the forepeak; but the repairs stood the test even when we fired a broadside and that night I signaled to the Naval Staff, *"Am resuming operations. Maintenance of high speed possible except in bad weather. Request permission to remain in Indian Ocean."* After further exhaustive tests, during which no more leaks opened up, we increased speed to fourteen knots, shaping course for the Australian shipping lanes where I proposed to extend the range of our operations by using the seaplane for reconnaissance.

On January 18—the anniversary of the foundation of the *Reich*—the German radio broadcast a propaganda speech scoffing at "the cowardice and inefficiency of the British Navy, which so far had not succeeded in preventing the operations of a single German commerce raider." The indignation over this speech among my ship's company was as great as my own; whatever people at home might be feeling, the last thing we wanted was to galvanize the British into making any greater efforts in our direction.

In a signal commenting on the *Atlantis*'s war diaries that Kamenz had brought home, the Naval Staff laid stress once again on the importance of "not overestimating the danger of being D/F'd when transmitting." The Naval Staff maintained that it was perfectly safe to send short signals from the South Atlantic and the Indian Ocean; I thought that such optimistic views were highly dangerous. Late in the evening of January 19, when we were on the Capetown-India route, we intercepted a signal from the *Pinguin* in the Weddell Sea in the Antarctic. She had captured two whaling factory-ships, the *Solglimt* and *Pelagos,* the tanker *Ole Wegger* and eleven whale catchers. This was success on the grand scale.

A few days later we found ourselves once more on the *Automedon*'s old course and sent off our seaplane to reconnoitre. As soon as she returned—with her port float slightly damaged—we turned north. The pilot had reported sighting a westbound ship sixty miles to the north of us.

16

NEW TACTICS

So much alarm had been created by the shelling of Nauru that I decided to make sure of this ship's identity before letting her see us. The first thing we sighted was a thick black cloud of smoke, suggesting that she was a coal burner—and therefore less likely to be an auxiliary cruiser. I took *Atlantis* in two wide circles to allow the target to get ahead of me; I was afraid to stop engines lest on restarting they should emit a telltale black puff of exhaust gases. In considering whether to attack by day or by night I realized that in daylight the target would almost certainly turn away and make a distress signal; on the other hand, darkness fell so quickly in these latitudes—we were once more north of the equator, between the Seychelles and the Chagos Archipelago—that we might easily lose contact in a night attack, especially as the British Admiralty had ordered all ships to alter course 90 degrees at each dawn and dusk.

I decided to try a daylight approach first, since if this did not succeed, I could always come up with her in the dark. Little did I think that the pursuit of this ship was going to cost me two days and the loss of my aircraft. It was a long time since those early days when the *Scientist* had had to alter course to avoid ramming us. All Allied ships knew nowadays that even the tip of a masthead sighted on the horizon was sufficient justification to turn away; and if the stranger showed signs of approaching nearer, a signal must be made at once on the assumption that she was hostile.

Soon after I had taken my decision, the target showed that she was following the British Admiralty's orders to the letter. When she sighted us—still more than twelve miles away—she turned to starboard. We in our turn altered to port, hoping that this maneuver would be interpreted by the other ship as a sign of our obedience to the same orders. During our approach we had been able to see something of her; she was armed—we could see at least two guns—and had the look of an English ship. As we had expected, she reverted to her original course as soon as she saw us turn away. The range was now more than eighteen miles, so we were also able to turn back on our old course—a deception course for Cape Guardafui—without arousing her suspicions. We continued to steam parallel with the ship, whose masthead was just visible from our own—at the extreme range of our vision—and worked out an interception course to bring us up with her that night. This could not be plotted accurately as there were times when all we could see was the ship's smoke, and we also had to reckon with possible alterations in her course and speed between then and dusk.

At dusk however, we shaped course to intercept and went to action stations. The night came down inky black and still. According to our dead reckoning we should sight her exactly one hour after dark—but we didn't. We plotted alternative positions but again without success, and at length I reduced the degree of readiness for action and allowed half the hands to fall out. My only chance now lay in following the enemy's presumed course until daybreak, when it might be possible to reestablish contact.

When morning came and the horizon was still empty, we launched the seaplane; the pilot found the ship again twenty-five miles to the north. There seemed little point in waiting for nightfall before making our second approach, and in any case we were getting dangerously near the patrol areas of South African land-based aircraft. I sent for Bulla and told him I wanted to try a new plan.

"We are now just out of sight of the enemy, on his port side and on a parallel course," I said. "I am going to repeat my approach tactics of yesterday, though probably from a different direction. I want you to approach him from up-sun and try to pull his aerial down. You will do this on receipt of a radio signal from me, when the enemy is turning away at our approach and his attention is riveted on us. You will also attack with bombs and machine guns to stop him from getting up an emergency aerial. Do you think you can do that?"

"Yes, sir," said Bulla, "anyway, I can try."

I told him that a motorboat with spare bombs and ammunition would be lowered for him to replenish from; after the attack was over he could land close to it and we would pick him up there.

Bulla took off a few minutes later with two bombs, magazines fully loaded and enough fuel for one hundred minutes flying. Everything went according to plan. Just as the enemy ship turned away from us at full speed, Bulla launched a surprise attack on her out of the sun. He managed to do what he had always failed to do previously and tore down the enemy's aerial; he dropped his 100 lb. bombs close alongside and raked the bridge and funnel, and then the ship's AA guns when they tried ineffectually to answer his fire. We were coming up at full speed and I was expecting to hear at any moment the usual report, "Enemy is transmitting. Permission to open fire?" But this time it never came. For some extraordinary reason, no report was made from my main W/T office. All that could be deduced was that the enemy was replying to the aircraft's fire and was beginning to zigzag. I found out afterward that the pilot's signals were mutilated and incomplete; the auxiliary W/T office had picked them up correctly but had failed to pass them on. I suppose no amount of training will ever ensure the elimination of human weakness.

Eventually came the unwelcome report that the enemy was sending a distress signal, *"QQQ* Mandasor *in position . . . bombed from raider."* She was not yet within range of our guns. Bulla had broken off his attack after using up all his ammunition and had flown away. I ordered the flaps to be opened but I delayed opening fire. The enemy repeated his signal, *"QQQ* Mandasor *chased by raider and bombed.* Mandasor *chased and bombed by merchant ship raider."* Our W/T office sent an "acknowledgment" to confuse the enemy wireless operator, "Mandasor *from FBP Colombo RRRR understood."* But the *Mandasor* signaled again, *"QQQ chased and bombed by merchant ship raider bombed by his aircraft destroyed aerial by line thrown from plane."*

Then we came within range and turned hard a-starboard to bring all guns to bear. Our second salvo landed on the target and the ship's transmissions ceased; but instead of heaving-to, the *Mandasor* continued to zigzag and was obviously trying to avoid the fall of our shells, so we had to go on shooting until fire broke out amidships and she started to swing out her boats. As soon as we saw that she had stopped, though without heaving-to, we ceased fire.

On the way over to the burning ship, our search party picked several survivors out of the water, including the master who had put up such a stout resistance, and some colored men. She was burning so fiercely amidships that communications between her bows and stern could only be carried on by boat.

The *Mandasor* was a 5,144-ton ship belonging to the Brocklebank Co. of Liverpool; she was on her way from Calcutta to England via Durban. Once again we were able to salvage the ship's secret papers, charts and logs. We also got a lot of valuable stores off her, including food and some machine guns. The ship had been badly damaged by our shelling; she had had two hits in the forecastle, the foremast had been broken in two, two shells had hit the bridge, two amidships and one aft. The crew's quarters were a mass of flames which were gradually spreading to the cargo of jute in No. 4 hold.

Her master told me that he had heard in Calcutta how the raider which had captured the *Automedon* had run in very close, which was why he had turned right away on sighting us and had watched us out of sight before resuming his course at ten knots. As I was escorting him to the door of my cabin, he turned and said hesitatingly: "Captain, about 400 miles off Colombo I was stopped by the British auxiliary cruiser *Ranchi*."

"Yes," I said, "I believe that the *Ranchi* is on patrol between Ceylon and Sumatra. You wrote that in your log. Thank you, Captain."

And in fact his log for December 5 read, ". . . unknown vessel, white ensign, (P & O) name signaled."

My conversations with captured skippers often revealed the existence of very human failings among our enemies. I remember asking one of them one day: "How do you make your report to the NCSO (Naval Control Service Officer) when you arrive, Captain?"

He grinned. "I usually call on him at gin-time," he said, "between 6 and 7 in the evening. He is in a hurry to get to his club and says, '*Must* you come at this time? You didn't sight anything, did you?' I always say 'No' and he is happy because otherwise we would both have to fill out endless questionnaires in fourteen copies."

I laughed at that and told him that very much the same thing happened with us.

Another time I asked, "What is it like to sail in convoy?" My prisoner thought for some time and then answered slowly: "The worst part of it is when the ship ahead or astern of you is hit and you are not allowed to stop and help. The last ship in the convoy has orders to pick up survivors but even she is not allowed to stop. With your experience you can imagine what it feels like to be in such a position."

But to return to the *Mandasor*. Time was getting short, and I called for the transfer of stores to be speeded up. It would be dark at 7:30 and we had to scuttle the ship and then search for the aircraft, which was two hours steaming from us. I certainly did not want to be overtaken by darkness before I had gotten the plane and motorboat safely on board.

I laughed at that and told him that very much the same thing happened with us.

Another time I asked, "What is it like to sail in convoy?" My prisoner thought for some time and then answered slowly: "The worst part of it is when the ship ahead or astern of you is hit and you are not allowed to stop and help. The last ship in the convoy has orders to pick up survivors but even she is not allowed to stop. With your experience you can imagine what it feels like to be in such a position."

But to return to the *Mandasor*. Time was getting short, and I called for the transfer of stores to be speeded up. It would be dark at 7:30 and we had to scuttle the ship and then search for the aircraft, which was two hours steaming from us. I certainly did not want to be overtaken by darkness before I had got the plane and motorboat safely on board.

Unknown to me, the plane was in serious difficulties. The pilot had had to make a pancake landing and then taxi over to the motorboat, whose engine had gone dead. The rising wind swamped the plane's port float and the aircraft capsized. Her crew had been picked up and were waiting for our arrival, feeling very seasick in the wildly tossing boat.

At 4:20 P.M. we fired the scuttling charges and six minutes later the *Mandasor* had gone down by the bows, covering the sea with floating chests of tea from her cargo. As soon as she had gone, we set off in haste to find the plane and the motorboat; but when we got there, all that we could see was the boat with her crew and the airmen, who were glad to feel the deck beneath their feet again. The plane was half under water and with a heavy heart I ordered it to be sunk by gunfire. Its loss was all the more exasperating because it could have been avoided, and in the prevailing weather the plane could have been used almost every day. Under peacetime conditions it would have been written off as no longer airworthy by the autumn of 1940, so it was all the more remarkable that it had taken such an active part in the capture of no less than three ships, the *Ole Jacob, Benarty* and *Mandasor*.

On January 27, after four uneventful days, a lookout sighted a cloud of smoke followed by three funnels. I promptly turned away and ran off at fifteen knots. From the shape of her funnels and upper works, the ship was probably the *Queen Mary*. We could not make out whether she was in convoy, but in any case pursuit was out of the question as she was superior to us not only in speed but probably in armament as well. I was fully conscious of the wave of disappointment that ran through the ship as I gave my orders to the quartermaster and chief engineer. I cut right through the crew's grumblings by saying: "Does anyone really think that the British would allow such a valuable ship to sail unescorted? There's sure to be a cruiser beyond her which we cannot see." As a matter of fact, one of the British skippers said in casual conversation that evening that the *Queen Mary* was indeed being used as a transport in those waters, always escorted by a light cruiser. (After the war I learned that she was not the *Queen Mary*, but the 22,281-ton *Strathaird* of the P & O line, operating as a troop transport.) After changing direction several times I reverted in the evening to my original course. I headed for the route taken by tankers going to and from the Persian Gulf, planning to cruise around a point where the Naval Staff had said that the tanker routes intersected. On the evening of January 31 we sighted a masthead but no accompanying smoke. A dim shadow appeared on the horizon exactly at the time we had calculated. "Open the flaps!" How often had I given that order—and yet it was always followed by a momentary quickening of the pulse and a dry feeling in my throat. "Range 23,400 yards," called the gunnery officer and then, "Range 14,000 yards." We were coming up at fourteen knots. The moon, in its first quarter, had risen and visibility was good, with a slight haze on the skyline; then the moon suddenly disappeared and for some time we could see nothing. I altered towards the target and increased speed. Then we saw her; she had turned away, so she had obviously sighted us.

Our first salvo screamed over to her. "Illuminate the target!" In the glare of our searchlight there appeared a merchant ship of medium size and typically British build—her gun was not manned. After our third salvo she appeared to stop and I sounded the "cease fire" on the siren. I signaled on our smaller searchlight, *Stop. Do not use your wireless. Remain on board and await my boat. What ship?* Back came the reply, *"S—P—E—Y—B—A—N—K."* Lloyd's Register showed that the *Speybank* was a ship of 5,144 tons, owned by the Bank Line of Glasgow, where she had been built in 1926.

The search party returned with seventeen white prisoners. The captured ship was quite undamaged and —which was more important—had sent no distress signal. On first sighting the raider, Captain Morrow had assumed that she was a passenger ship on almost the same course as his own and had only made a slight turn to allow her to pass in safety. His first impressions appeared to be confirmed when *Atlantis* did not turn toward him, and he soon resumed his course. Even when the "passenger ship" suddenly appeared out of the darkness on his port quarter the idea of her being a raider never occurred to him, and he only steered more to the south to avoid a collision. He was on the point of signaling us to pay more attention and had stopped to avoid a collision when he was overtaken by *Atlantis*'s fire. He had promptly abandoned all thought of resistance in order to avoid loss of life.

The *Speybank* had sailed from Cochin on January 25 bound for New York; she was fully stored for the round trip. Her cargo included manganese ore, monazite, ilmenite and teak. I realized at once that here was indeed a valuable catch. Being fully stocked, the ship was well fitted to be a prize and her cargo would be of incalculable benefit to our war economy. As a typically British-looking vessel she was ideally suited as an auxiliary under a German flag. I ordered Breuers with a prize crew of ten men to take the ship to a rendezvous on the edge of the Malha Bank in position 10° south, 63° east. This capture brought our total to 104,101 tons of shipping.

The *Speybank* sailed off soon after midnight, while we resumed our search along the India route.

17

A MEETING WITH THE *SCHEER*

At 8:25 P.M. the next evening our guns were firing again. For the past seven hours we had been tracking down a medium-sized tanker. Now, as our searchlight came on, we could see that wild panic had broken out on board her. She did not answer our signals and her decks were swarming with men carrying torches. Then her deck lighting was switched on and she stopped without wirelessing or making any attempt to resist. We could see that she carried no gun—the first unarmed ship we had encountered. Her boats were low-

ered so hastily and inexpertly that two of them capsized; my order to remain on board was neither acknowledged nor obeyed, but someone was flashing SOS
from her stern. An upturned boat lay on her weather
side, its occupants clinging to the gunwales or hanging
on to the lifelines and falls. Another boat dropped into
the water and managed to stay upright.

As the tanker had not wirelessed and had stopped
at once, we ceased fire after the third salvo and I sent
away the boarding party. They reached her to find blind
panic still reigning; most of her crew, mainly Chinese,
were still on board but at first the master could not be
found anywhere—events had completely unbalanced
him. Norwegians and Chinese, many of whom had
climbed back on board from the overturned boats, were
running blindly around the decks, carrying their possessions in bags and bundles. High-pressure steam was
escaping with a deafening roar from a broken pipe
aft. The bridge was untenanted and in darkness. Some
of the ship's papers were finally located by the light of
a flashlight. The tanker was the *Ketty Brovig*, 7,031
tons, built in 1918 and registered in Farsund; she was
en route from Aswali in Bahrein to Lourenço Marques
with a cargo of oil fuel and diesel oil. She had a crew of
nine Norwegians and forty-three Chinese. The diesel
oil would keep *Atlantis* going for a long time. It was
doubtful if we would be able to get the ship under way
again, as a shell had pierced the main steam pipe just
above the main valve and it could not be repaired
until the boilers had died down. This meant losing all
the boiler water; the boiler water feed pump and the
fuel pumps could only be driven by steam, but steam
was only forthcoming if boiler water and fuel could be
pumped in. As there were very few hand pumps on
board, the prize crew appeared to have an insoluble
problem on their hands.

As a preliminary measure we provided some
spares and a "saddle-piece" from our workshops to
stop the leak in the *Ketty*'s steampipe. Some of the
Norwegians and Chinese were transferred, the rest remained under the orders of Lieutenant Fehler as prize
captain. A few of them, including the first mate, kept

on explaining excitedly that the ship was bound for a neutral port; whereupon they were asked why the ship had been steaming without lights or visible nationality markings and was painted gray all over. When asked to produce the ship's papers in support of their claim that they were bound for Lourenço Marques, their statement that the master had thrown them overboard —together with £700 in cash—was received with polite disbelief. The master himself, Captain Moeller, took no part in these arguments.

After some hours we managed to mend the broken pipe and the fires were relighted to raise steam. The fuel pumps were still out of order, but the repair party managed to isolate the steam-filled boiler and thus save some of the precious water in it. I decided to leave the tanker at dawn and ordered Fehler to wait for me until February 18 at a rendezvous known as "Oak Tree."

Two days later I made a report to Berlin. First I sent a brief signal, *"Have sunk 111,000 tons. Speed fourteen knots. Am proceeding to rendezvous-position Carnation";* and then in greater detail, *"Ketty Brovig with 4,000 tons of diesel 32.6 APL, 6,000 tons oil fuel and Speybank with teak, manganese, monazite, tea, sailed for Carnation. Propose to refuel Speybank from Ketty and send her home as prize."* I continued with a request that a meeting be arranged with the *Kormoran* and the pocket battleship *Admiral Scheer,* which had recently switched her operational area from the South Atlantic to the Indian Ocean; and I finished with a report that *Atlantis* was "fully operational and ready to continue to the limit of her endurance." I wanted to guard against being recalled prematurely and I asked for directives in the Atlantic, my next operational area.

The *Ketty Brovig* was the last ship we captured in the Indian Ocean, for we now received orders to rendezvous with the *Tannenfels* and the Italian submarine *Perla,* both coming from Italian Somaliland and in need of supplies. Our own supply arrangements were far from perfect! We learned that part of the stores destined for us had been loaded by mistake in the supply ship *Alsterufer* instead of the *Alstertor,* and that we should have to have them delivered by the *Nordmark;* food supplies for two months allocated for the *Thor* and *Atlantis* had not been given separate markings, so the two ships would have to share them out equally. The Naval Staff did not consider the *Ketty Brovig*'s diesel oil suitable for the *Admiral Scheer,* so *Atlantis* was ordered to replenish the *Scheer* from her own bunkers and take over the *Ketty*'s oil herself, after which the *Ketty* was to proceed to position "Siberia." We met the *Speybank* as arranged on February 8 and after taking on stores from her, I ordered her to steer for position "Pineapple"; at noon on Monday February 10 the *Tannenfels* came in sight in position "Persia," after the careless deciphering of a signal had caused her to wait for three days near "Persia" on the wrong latitude. Her hull was very foul from lying in harbor for so many months and she stood very high out of the water because the Italians had refused to let her sail until she had unloaded a part of her cargo of jute, worth some five million Reichsmarks. She was now so light that her propeller was half out of the water; her chances of posing as a UK-bound ship were thus lessened by the appearance of being in ballast— a most unlikely state of affairs in view of the shortage of Allied shipping.

Lieutenant Dehnel and the *Durmitor*'s prize crew rejoined us from the *Tannenfels* and I was amazed to hear the full story of their fantastic journey. He told me that the Italian authorities—the Navy foremost among them—had placed every sort of obstacle in their way. As the *Durmitor*'s coal supplies had given out halfway to Somaliland, she had been abandoned at Chisimaio, and Dehnel and his men had sought safety in the *Tannenfels* from the rapid advance of the British troops. Dehnel's report on conditions in the Italian colony confirmed my worst fears—everywhere there was rampant inefficiency, apathy and complete lack of cooperation. Besides the *Pennsylvania,* loaded with diesel oil, there were fifteen other ships in Chisimaio, including a fast banana ship and some tankers which could have been of the greatest value as supply ships for our raiders; but nobody had taken the slightest trouble to exploit these possibilities.

However, I had little time to worry about such shortcomings, for I now had no fewer than three satellite ships to look after; I could not help wondering whether we were supposed to be an auxiliary warship or a floating ship's chandlery. We had to refuel the *Speybank* from our own bunkers, replace the *Ketty Brovig*'s prize crew with Dehnel and the ex-*Durmitor* men, distribute the civilians from the *Tannenfels* among the other ships, put our prisoners into her and provide food for all three ships. While we gave the *Storstadt*'s oil to the *Speybank,* we ourselves took over the high-quality oil from the *Ketty;* we also shared our lifeboats and provided each ship with flags, chronometers, sextants, charts, medicine, paint, wire logs and tobacco. All this had to be worked out in the minutest detail as we only had two days in which to do it. On February 13 my little squadron of four ships got under way to meet the *Admiral Scheer*.

The weather steadily deteriorated, with heavy seas and poor visibility. I had refrained from telling my crew of the intended meeting with the battleship, so there was considerable tension when, at noon on February 14, the lookouts reported, "Warship on the port bow!" However, when they saw that I was not unduly perturbed, my men looked again and on recognizing the *Scheer,* their anxiety turned to wild excitement. The crew of the *Scheer,* who at first thought they had come upon a convoy, were almost disappointed to find that the ships were only *Atlantis* and her satellites. As soon as I found that the *Scheer* had no prisoners on board, I sailed the *Tannenfels* for Europe. She reached Bordeaux without mishap on April 19—sixteen days ahead of schedule—with five men acting as guards over forty-two Englishmen and sixty-one colored men.

On the first day of our meeting, the tail of a tropical hurricane swept over the ships and it was only with the greatest difficulty that I managed to make my way over in the captured Norwegian motorcutter to pay a short visit to the *Scheer*. Later the same day all ships, led by the *Scheer,* got under way to seek calmer seas further to the north. The *Ketty* was unable to maintain her speed, lost station during the night and was only located again two days later.

The *Scheer* took from the *Ketty Brovig* all the oil she could hold; although the Naval Staff had declared it unsuitable for the battleship, her chief engineer was delighted with it. We handed over our mail to be posted at home and parties of all ranks exchanged visits between the two ships. I was particularly glad of the opportunuity of exchanging news with the *Scheer's* captain. It was so long since I had been able to talk with someone of the same rank, with whom I could discuss my problems freely and frankly and from whom I could get sound advice. I valued his comments and I listened eagerly as he brought me up to date in affairs at home, the progress of the war on land and at sea, and Germany's economic position. Time passed all too quickly in such pleasant circumstances. Not a day had passed since we left harbor without the knowledge that death—in the shape of an enemy warship—might be lurking below the horizon; it was very comforting to have the *Scheer's* gray bulk looming over us. One of my ratings gazed admiringly at her big guns and the radar endlessly sweeping the horizon and murmured, "Last night I slept really soundly." He spoke for us all.

Two days later we were alone again. By arrangement with the *Scheer's* captain I cruised from February 17 to 25 south of the Seychelles along the *Mandasor's* route, and thence east toward the Chagos Archipelago, while the *Scheer* patrolled southwest of the Seychelles along the routes we had discovered. I used the *Speybank* to enlarge my patrol area, sending her out as a scout thirty miles on my flank, whence she could report by a specially arranged signal. Breuers, her captain, was able to maintain contact with us in a new and very remarkable way, by taking bearings on the radiations of our radio receiver. Although the experts said this was impossible, subsequent developments proved that Breuers was only too right. He achieved his first success on February 20, when he sighted a medium-sized tanker and maintained contact with her out of sight; *Atlantis* then took over and I sent Breuers off to wait for me at a rendezvous. I kept contact all day without a doubt as to our eventual success, but at dusk the tanker put on her lights and soon afterward we saw two more lights very low down, quite near her. We approached cautiously and after an exchange of signals we confirmed that this was the French naval tanker *Lot* and two submarines about which we had been warned by signal from the Naval Staff. Next there appeared beyond the French squadron the lights of some ships steaming in line ahead which looked like torpedo boats. We withdrew without challenging them and next day we closed the *Speybank* to give her fresh orders.

Two hours later she reported another ship, this time of 5,000 tons. I sent the *Speybank* to join the *Ketty Brovig* off the Saya de Malha Bank, where the supply ship *Uckermark* should also have arrived, and, as on the previous day, took station some thirty miles away from the merchant ship—now reported as a Blue Funnel liner. I intended to attack her after dark but once again we suffered a disappointment. As night fell the ship switched on her lights and in answer to our challenge identified herself as the Japanese *S.S. Africa Maru*. We had wasted nine hours on her. Then the *Speybank* reported that the *Uckermark* had not turned up, so we steered for our second rendezvous with the *Scheer*, only to be met, to our surprise, not by the battleship herself but by a prize she had captured, from whom we learned that the *Scheer* had had to start for home. After refueling from the tanker *Nordmark* in the Atlantic, the *Scheer* reached Kiel on April 1. Her prize, the tanker *British Advocate*, was the first of three she had captured in the Indian Ocean.

Supplying the *British Advocate* was a thankless task. Her prize crew appeared to have been selected from the most useless members of the *Scheer*'s company; they were largely dependent upon the goodwill of the tanker's crew. The working of the ship was left entirely in British hands while the prize crew, armed with pistols, lounged around doing nothing. They were more of a hindrance than a help to our working party and when even Fehler could not get any sense out of them, I myself had to intervene. After stocking her up I sailed the *British Advocate* to Bordeaux where—contrary to all our expectations—she arrived without incident on April 29. On March 21 we met the *Speybank* for the last time and prepared her for the voyage home. In place of the experienced Breuers I put her under the command of young Sub-Lieutenant Schneidewind, formerly first mate of the *Tannenfels*. He later carried out a minelaying mission in her off Capetown with the utmost coolness and resource. On May 10 the *Speybank* arrived in Bordeaux with her valuable cargo.

We then sailed to rendezvous with the Italian submarine *Perla,* but she failed to materialize. When at last we made contact by D/F, we found that the *Perla* was lying one hundred and twenty miles south of the correct position, due to a "slight error of judgment" on the part of the Italian Naval Staff. The Italian crew was obviously in low spirits after their long period of inactivity in Massawa under constant bombing from the air and the steady stream of setbacks on all Italian fronts. They had some remarkable ideas on how the war should be fought. The commanding officer himself told me that he always dived the moment a masthead was sighted. He was proposing to steer one hundred and fifty miles south of Capetown; he considered it far too dangerous to send any signals in the Indian Ocean and had not attempted to make a single attack, although the emergence of a U-boat off the coast of South Africa would obviously make a most valuable impression on the enemy.

His submarine was in a pitiable condition. Her CO had only a homemade chart on board and we had to supply her with all sorts of things besides seventy tons of fuel and food. After some hesitation her captain agreed to operate in company with me off South Africa until April 8; he was to patrol off Durban while we searched the Mozambique Channel and the shipping lanes two hundred miles from the coast. It transpired subsequently that the CO had thought this too risky, for we never heard from him again. We heard instead a triumphant announcement that "Mussolini had received some Italian submarine commanders from the Red Sea and had congratulated them and their crews on their exemplary conduct and courage." I was awarded the *Medaglia di Bronzo al Valor Militar* (the Bronze Medal for Military Valor, corresponding to the British Distinguished Service Cross) for the "gallant assistance and comradeship that had been extended to an Italian warship."

On March 31 we completed our first year at sea. The commander-in-chief signaled his congratulations and good wishes and besides awarding several Iron Crosses, First Class, he conferred the Second Class on the entire ship's company. On April 8, 1941, we left the Indian Ocean after spending nearly twelve months in it. I summarized our activities in my log as follows:

"Conditions have changed greatly since we arrived in May, 1940. In the early months the only effect on shipping movements of our operations was that the routes from the Cape to Colombo and Sabang were spaced out more widely. It was not until the beginning of 1941 that any significant changes were made, when the main shipping route was diverted through the Mozambique Channel and an increasing amount of Australian traffic was sent via Panama. Apart from troop transports no convoys were formed except on the route through the Red Sea to Bombay, where shipping came within range of attacks launched from Italian territory. To the direct success we have achieved—the sinking of fifteen ships of more than 100,000 tons aggregate, often with most valuable cargo—should be added the indirect effect on the trade war, such as the tying down of warships and the diversion of merchant ships nearer the coast, which must have resulted in a higher consumption of fuel and a slower turnaround of the ships. Ships have been compelled to zigzag on moonlight nights and in daytime, ports have been blacked out, lighthouses have been extinguished, booms have been raised at night, even ships that were only working in the Indian ocean have had to be defensively armed, and alarm and despondency has spread among native populations. Ships' crews have been paid danger money even in the Indian Ocean and the recruiting of crews in the colonies has been impeded. Navigation in narrow coastal waters has been made more difficult, mails have been unreliable and official despatches have been lost. War insurance rates have risen, the need for extra personnel on ships and in coastal radio stations has caused a drain on manpower, and the enemy has had to send defense units to East Africa and Indian seaports and to allocate mine-sweeping flotillas to them.

"Another result of our campaign is that British and Allied merchant skippers have taken added precautions and are much readier to obey the British Admiralty directives. This has meant that our earlier tactics of gradually closing on our victims by day and of firing a shot across their bows have had to give way to surprise attacks by night. There have been several stages in this development. First we tried to stop a ship by firing a round across her bows from the 7.5 cm gun; then we used the 6 inch, then half a 6 inch salvo, then a full salvo over the target, and when even this failed to impress the enemy sufficiently, we opened fire with all guns directly on the target, without warning and at the closest possible range.

"Craft and cunning have played an all-important part but although trickery proved successful in two cases—the *Ole Jacob* and the *Teddy*—it can only be used under special circumstances and must always be new and unexpected. In all circumstances I have tried to make war in accordance with the old raider tradition of 'fairness,' by which I mean that where possible I never fired for longer than was absolutely necessary to break down the enemy's resistance and destroy his wireless. Where we had a chance of identifying the ship as a tanker or a particularly valuable prize and could take a chance on her sending a distress signal, we refrained from opening fire. We have treated our prisoners and survivors as we would wish to be treated ourselves in similar circumstances; we have tried to make their lot as easy as possible."

18

THE *ZAM ZAM'S* PASSENGERS

On April 8, 1941, we had reached latitude 41°
south, south of the Cape of Good Hope, on our way to
meet the supply ship *Alsterufer* which had left Hamburg in January; after that we were due to rendezvous
with the *Dresden* and *Babitonga* coming from South
America, and finally with the U-boat supply ship *Nordmark,* which had embarked Captain Kamenz after his
journey around the world. A meeting had also been
planned with the raider *Kormoran.*

As we had been delayed by our meeting with the
Perla, the *Alsterufer* had been sent off far to the south
and so the first ship we met, also four days behind
schedule, was the Lloyd liner *Dresden* which, after acting as supply ship for the *Graf Spee,* had sought sanc-
tuary in Santos, Brazil. I was delighted to see Captain
Jäger of the *Dresden* as he was due to give us some
much needed supplies of fresh food, but he looked unhappy as we shook hands.

"I'm afraid I have a disappointment for you," he
said. "I embarked your fresh food all right but then I
got instructions from our Naval Attaché to hand them
over to the *Babitonga,* although she has no cold room.
Both her captain and I pointed out that with a temperature of 104 degrees, the fresh food would undoubtedly
go bad in her holds, but we were simply told to obey
orders."

I was livid with rage. After months at sea, we
were desperately in need of fresh fruit, vegetables
and potatoes; our vitamin tablets were becoming steadily less effective and the crew's health was suffering. The

Dresden could have preserved the fruit and vegetables in perfect condition in her cold room, but she had been prevented from doing so by a piece of bureaucratic and high-handed stupidity that merited heavy punishment. The only fresh food that the *Dresden* could give us were potatoes, and these were handed over during the day together with lubricant, fresh water and timber. We also took on reinforcements to the ship's company in the shape of two individuals calling themselves Meyer and Müller, who soon identified themselves as former members of the sunken *Graf Spee*. Meyer, whose real name was Fröhlich, had been given commissioned rank in recognition of his outstanding services in the presence of the enemy as senior wireless operator in the pocket battleship; the other man was a prize officer called Sub-Lieutenant (S) Dittmann. Both men chose to transfer to *Atlantis* instead of returning home in the *Dresden,* although they had been serving without a break since August, 1939.

After embarking the *Dresden*'s stores, I told her captain to wait at a pre-arranged position until I had ascertained whether the *Kormoran* had any prisoners to dispose of. Little did I think that within eight hours I myself would have more prisoners on my hands than I liked, including a large number of the kind that I would rather not have seen at all—American women and children.

At about four o'clock in the morning, barely an hour after we had parted from the *Dresden,* we sighted a fairly large ship on a southeasterly course. She was completely blacked-out but in the brilliant moonlight was easily identified as a merchant ship. Very soon we were able to make out four masts and I remembered having seen some ships of the same type in Dartmouth during the Coronation festivities before the war. I recalled the scene vividly. I had asked the British officer acting as my guide, "What are those four-masted ships over there—what do you use them for? Auxiliary cruisers?" He had replied: "Those are Bibby liners, troop transports from the Great War. We are still using them as such, for there are always troops that have

to be moved somewhere." I was sure that this was a
Bibby liner. She steamed so close to the *Dresden* that
the latter promptly turned tail and fled, while the Bibby
ship suddenly started to zigzag as though she had sighted
us and was trying to escape. It was only hours later
that we learned that there was no question of her trying
to flee—it was merely that her helmsman was an Egyptian!

Her size and suspicious movements made me wonder whether she was in fact being used as an auxiliary
cruiser, and as we followed cautiously in her wake, I
made up my mind to get within range of her at daybreak and make a surprise attack. I wanted at all costs
to prevent her from sending an SOS, as the South Atlantic was narrower and better patrolled than our previous operational area; our only hope was to attack with
every gun that would bear. My plans had to be expe-
dited when the ship began to transmit a signal—quite
a harmless one at first, *"What station is that?"*—but
we could not know whether her next one would be
"QQQ" or "RRR." The ship was now standing out
clearly against the early morning sky and we identified
her definitely as one of the *Oxfordshire* class, though
we still could not see whether she was armed nor could
we distinguish the colors of her ensign. I hesitated no
longer and at 9,200 yards opened fire. The second
salvo was on target and one shell smashed the wireless
cabin; she was hit six times in all, sustaining heavy
damage on the waterline and in the engine room. The
ship at first turned away, then stopped, blew off steam
and lowered her boats. She made no SOS signal—her
wireless cabin was a heap of ruins. We ceased fire.

Here is how one of my officers afterward described
the scene:

> "Day was breaking as *Atlantis* approached
> the enemy ship; the first rays of the sun shone on
> the gently heaving swell where the ship lay with a
> heavy list. She was the *Zam Zam*, 8,299 tons,
> previously known as a Bibby Line troop trans-
> port under the name of *Leicestershire* and later
> as the *British Exhibitor;* for some years she had

been serving as the largest ship in the Egyptian merchant navy. Boats were drifting about everywhere, some fully laden, others floating keel upward. People were clinging on to them. Some of the boats were only half full; thin brown men with terror-stricken faces were squatting in them —the Egyptian crew, who had rushed for the boats without bothering about the passengers. As the German motorboats moved toward the *Zam Zam* they let out wild cries for help, but the Germans paid no attention, being intent on rescuing first the women and children and those who had been left on board the badly damaged ship.

"It was no easy task. The shark-infested waters were full of men and women swimming about. One mother had taken off her life jacket and put her little son on it; holding him on with her hands, she was struggling toward the boats. It was a miracle that nobody was drowned. The scene on board the *Zam Zam* was shocking. All the boats on the port side were still hanging from the wrecked davits, riddled with shell holes. The great mirrors in the dining saloon and smoking room had been shattered and the tables hurled in all directions. Big black holes gaped where the shells had exploded.

"While in Trinidad, the *Zam Zam* had received orders from the British Admiralty to follow a prearranged course across the Atlantic. The master's request to be allowed to steam with his lights burning at night because of the presence of women and children on board had been refused; the ship was carrying a British cargo and therefore had to conform to the regulations. Among the two hundred and two passengers were seventy-seven women and thirty-two children; one hundred and forty of them were American, the rest were nationals of Canada, Belgium and various other countries. Amazingly enough, our shelling had not caused the loss of a single life and with the exception of three serious casualties, no one was hurt. This miraculous escape was attributed to very different causes by the Christian missionaries and by those of the Moslem faith (*Zam Zam* is the name of a holy well in Mecca).

"The working parties did their best to transfer all the passengers' luggage, the fresh food, tobacco, crockery, mattresses and blankets, for the ship had a heavy list and was filling rapidly as water rushed through the shell hole in the engine room. The boats that returned empty from *Atlantis* were quickly filled with articles of clothing and trunks seized at random from the upper deck cabins; armfuls of coats and trousers were snatched from cupboards and flung into the waiting launches. As the last boat came alongside, laden to the gunwale, the raider's decks looked like a gypsy's caravan or an emigrant ship. The passengers crowded together on the boat deck and watched the *Zam Zam* being sunk. Some of those who had come on board in their pajamas were bare-footed, wearing dressing gowns borrowed from the German officers. Children were shrieking, crying or laughing, mothers were wringing their hands, babes in arms were peering mutely at the confusion around them. The children were highly delighted with this new adventure; the grown-ups were less enthusiastic. Most of them had lost many of their possessions, some of them everything. The German officers were besieged with questions from all sides.

" 'Where can I get some milk? It's time for Susie to have her milk.'

" 'Can you tell me where the sick bay is? Perhaps I can find some nappies there?'

" 'Have you got lifejackets for all of us?'

" 'Can someone fetch my glasses and my manicure case? I left them in the ship. Cabin 237.'

" 'Where shall we sleep tonight?'

" 'When do you think we can get off this ship?'

" 'I would so like some iced orangeade. What! You haven't got any orangeade? How can you live without it? I couldn't subsist a week without my orangeade. You're joking, Lieutenant. Be a good boy and tell me where I can get some.'

"The officer looked the lady straight in the eye and summoned up his best English.

" 'Listen,' he said, 'I no longer remember what an orange looks like or tastes like. On this ship we live on dried potatoes, dried onions and dried fish—fortunately not only on dry bread.

The only wet thing, thank goodness, is the beer—
and Dr. Reil's whiskey and soda.'

" 'Oh really, and do you think we Americans
will also have to live on that?'

" 'I am afraid, yes.'

" 'And for a long time?'

"The same question was looming hugely before the captain of *Atlantis*. Three hundred extra
mouths to feed would soon wreck his calculations
of the raider's endurance. He thanked heaven
that the *Dresden* was available to take this human
freight off his hands."

On learning that there were more Americans
among the *Zam Zam*'s passengers than there had been
in the *Lusitania* in 1916, I realized at once that the
capture of this Egyptian ship could be turned to excellent account by that section of the American Press
which was trying to force the United States into the
war. Properly handled, the case of the *Zam Zam* could
be made into the *Lusitania* story of the Second World
War. It was therefore all the more important to impress
the Americans with our generosity and sense of chiv-
alry. As luck would have it among the passengers were
a traveling American journalist, Charles Murphy, editor of the magazine *Fortune* and a prominent contribu-
tor to *Time* and *Life,* and a *Life* photographer named
Scherman; it was certain that neither of them would
ignore the chance of making the most sensational scoop
of their lives. Murphy's eyewitness account of the capture and sinking of the *Zam Zam* would have the greatest influence on public opinion in the U.S.A. and might
in fact be used in support of the isolationist group.

By personal contact we managed to engender a
favorable atmosphere on board and to gain the passengers' cooperation. The missionaries were surprised
and delighted when we returned to them the chalice of
pure gold which they had forgotten in their headlong
flight. Within twenty-four hours they were able to
leave the raider and transfer to the *Dresden,* which was
then sent off to a waiting position for a week before
joining up with us again. Thanks to Captain Jäger's

tact and discretion, the passengers had managed by that time to settle down comfortably, but they had employed the intervening time to draw up a formal protest, as neutral citizens, against being exposed to a permanent risk, which would be increased if and when the *Dresden* attempted to break through the British blockade.

My intention was to transfer the Americans and all the women and children to the first neutral ship we encountered, or alternatively to send the *Dresden* to Las Palmas or Teneriffe in the Canary Islands; but the Naval Staff would not agree to this and the *Dresden* was ordered to make for Western France, where in fact she arrived on May 20, 1941. Two days before that—a full four weeks after the ship had been sunk—the British Admiralty announced that the *Zam Zam* had been overdue since April 21. The American Press's reaction was extraordinarily quick: "LINER ON PASSAGE TO AFRICA DISAPPEARS. 142 AMERICANS PERISH?" "The *Zam Zam* carried distinctive neutrality markings," said the *New York Times,* adding, "There are no waters undefiled by the Nazi pirates, no flag which they will respect. . . ." On the other hand there were newspapers which spoke of ". . . exemplary adherence to the prize regulations . . . no member of the crew nor any passengers lost their lives . . . it is being stressed in Washington that the German ship acted in accordance with the rules of war in taking passengers and crew on board before sinking a ship that was carrying contraband goods. . . ." At last, after many contradictory reports, there appeared in *Life* on June 23, 1941, an article by Charles Murphy on his experiences. Here are some extracts from it.

"The rickety Egyptian ship *Zam Zam,* bound from New York to Alexandria via the Cape of Good Hope, put into Baltimore on March 23 to take on additional cargo and passengers. There, Captain William Gray Smith looked down unhappily on the pier where one hundred and twenty missionaries sang *Lead Kindly Light,* and two dozen cheerful irreverent ambulance drivers tried to drown them out with an impudent song of their own. Smith, a bouncy little Scot with a weather-reddened face, turned to his chief engineer. 'Mark my words, Chief,' he said grimly, 'it's bad luck for a ship to have so many Bible punchers and sky pilots aboard. No good will come of this.'

"Scherman and I boarded the *Zam Zam* at Recife, having flown to Brazil to save time at sea. The *Zam Zam*, due April 1, arrived a week late. When we hurried down to the docks to confirm the miracle of her appearance, the rails were crowded with people clamoring to be left off. Some were shouting rude jibes at the dock workers. A passenger bellowed down at us: 'If you two intend to come aboard this wreck, don't ever say we didn't warn you what you're in for. The food's lousy, the crew's lousier.' He pointed toward the stack, where the word MISR, from the company's name, was visible. 'They even call her Misery Ship.'

"The *Zam Zam* put out for Capetown April 9, delayed for two hours by one of the table stewards, who had overslept in a brothel. Our presence raised the passenger list to two hundred and two, of whom seventy-three were women and thirty-five were children. There were one hundred and thirty-eight Americans, twenty-six Canadians, twenty-five British, five South Africans, four Belgians, one Italian, one Norwegian and two Greek nurses. The crew numbered one hundred and twenty-nine—one hundred and six Egyptians, nine Sudanese, six Greeks, two Yugoslavs, two Turks, one Czech, one French and two British—the captain and chief engineer. We headed past the breakwater shortly after 7 A.M. and from then until we were hit at dawn, eight days later, we never saw another ship . . . The *Zam Zam* was traveling without lights and in radio silence. She flew no flag and there were no identifying marks on her sides. Even the customary noon positions were denied the passengers. . . .

"Wednesday night, the 16, we were five days out of Capetown. It was pitch dark when I turned in just after midnight. I fell asleep almost instantly. The next thing I knew the air was trembling with a terrible vibration, a meaningless sound welling up around me. Scherman, already on his feet, was tearing at his camera case under the bed and yelling, 'Get up! Get up! They're shelling us!"

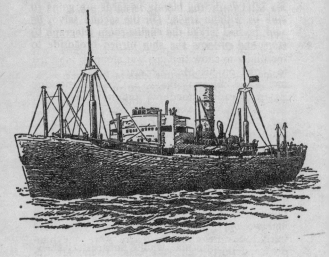

Atlantis

"A blind animal instinct drove me out of the cabin to the deck, on the starboard side, opposite the sun, which had not yet risen. From somewhere, quite near, came several loud reports. The atmosphere tightened into a tense, spiraling scream, and even as I shriveled against the bones of my body the water directly abeam, less than 100 yards away, rose up in two crackling columns and subsided. There was another salvo, after which the ship shook and trembled, and I heard a tearing, rending noise. In the dark—all the lights were out—I crossed over to the port side, and the moment I stepped out on deck I saw the German raider. She was broadside on, so close I could count her bridge decks, and if ever a ship looked the role, she did—a ship of ambush, very low in the water, black against the dawn. Even as I looked several long red flashes spurted forward and abaft the funnel, and as I raced back to the cabin the passageway behind me heaved and filled with smoke. That shot, I think, hit the lounge. I heard a child cry, and a hoarse, hurt voice screaming an Arabic oath . . . 'The thought came over me,' Captain Smith told me afterward, 'the bloody bastards are going to sink us without trace.' On the second salvo, he said, he had jerked the engine-room telegraph to stop, and ordered the ship turned broadside to the raider to show that she was stopped. He tried to signal on his Morse blinker, but shell fragments had cut away the wire. One of the young Egyptian cadets stood by, and he sent him to find a flashlight. About that time a shell struck the captain's bedroom fair, smashing the wall in, and sending a spray of splinters across the bridge. . . . Altogether, the firing lasted about ten minutes—from 5:55 to 6:05. Our estimates as to the number of shots fired ranged from twelve to twenty, but the German gunnery lieutenant on the raider later said he had fired fifty-five. If so, it was ragged shooting, considering the close range. At least nine shots went into the *Zam Zam*, all on the port side.

"After that brutal, wholly unnecessary shelling of an unarmed ship—a ship not only stopped but hopelessly stricken—I thought they'd slip alongside and put a torpedo into her. I pulled a pair of pants over my pajamas, put on shoes, grabbed up my topcoat, wallet and passport, and went to my lifeboat station.

"Let it be said for the crew that at least they got the boats over quickly and in good order. But let it also be said that once they themselves were safely in the boats, their behavior was abominable. They screamed and bellowed at the top of their lungs, they fought to pull away when the boats were only half full, and because we couldn't understand them nor they us we had a horrible time trying to control the boats. Mrs. Starling, plump and middle-aged, raced down a ladder to hold a boat for her wounded husband, whom three men had carried to the rail. Just as she reached the bottom of the ladder the boat pulled away, and not having the strength to climb back, she let go and fell into the water. Swept astern, she was paddling weakly when an ambulance driver hauled her onto a raft. . . .

"Within half an hour after the shelling all the boats were down and milling around the *Zam Zam*. The sea, except for a prolonged, easy swell, was calm. As our boat moved away I saw, with a sick feeling in the stomach, that dead astern of the *Zam Zam* the sea was full of bobbing heads. Two lifeboats, riddled with shell splinters, had filled almost as soon as they hit the water.

"After I had entirely forgotten about the Germans and was bitterly weighing the chances of this ragged flotilla ever reaching land, the raider surged around the *Zam Zam*'s stern, moving cautiously as if she feared a trap. Lines snaked over the side as she approached, but instead of securing them to the boat so that it could be pulled to the ladder as the Germans intended, the Egyptians tried to climb up hand over hand. The lines were torn loose and thrown forth again, with an angry command to make them fast. Again the Egyptians tried to save themselves. Afterward, a German officer told us they were about to shoot them off the lines when two motorboats, which had been lowered on the other side, came around the stern and picked up the people in the water.

"The raider stopped just below the line of boats, which were strung out about a quarter of a mile apart, and a voice in English bellowed at us through a megaphone: 'Come alongside, please. We are taking you aboard.' I had a good look at her then. She was about 8,000 tons, with a raised forecastle and a well deck aft. The hull was black, the housing and trim gray. As our boat came around the stern I saw her name *Tamesis* (Thames) and underneath it the port: Tonsberg. By that time only a stern gun, which we guessed to be a 6 incher, was visible. The others, during the half hour the raider lay watching us abandon ship, had been carefully concealed behind false work or lowered by hidden elevators below deck.

Sailors and marines in tropical whites and armed with rifles lined the rails.

"Germans at war waste no time on ceremony. As each boat pulled alongside the vertical ladder, we were ordered roughly but politely to come up and German sailors jumped down to help the women and children. Stretchers were lowered for the wounded. The small children went up in hemp baskets crying miserably. . . .

"All that morning we milled around the hatch. The crew had been herded aft and we had no contact with them. The sun blazed down and hungry children whimpered until the women were offered the shelter of the lower deck. All the while, the two motorboats shuttled back and forth carrying stuff to the raider from the *Zam Zam* which was abeam, listing heavily to port and looking strangely tranquil. This was looting —extremely efficient looting. An endless chain of German sailors passed the hatch, shouldering boxes of provisions, cigarettes, radios, photographs, suitcases, even a child's tricycle. Every now and then an excited, jubilant cry would come from one of the passengers as he or she recognized a prized belonging.

"Nobody told us anything. We just sat and watched—bumming cigarettes from the farsighted ones who had crammed extra packages into their pockets. That noon, volunteers brought food in metal bowls from the galley—a thick soup, together with lime juice. . . .

"That afternoon Lieutenant Mohr asked Captain Smith to choose three or four representative passengers whom Captain Rogge of the *Tamesis* could interview. I was one thus chosen. We were taken to the topside and ushered into a beautiful little room with a handsome table, upholstered settee, and hung with gay chintz curtains. Captain Rogge stood up and shook hands with us. He was a tall, strongly built, handsome man in the middle forties with wide-spaced eyes and beautiful manners. He was, I learned later, a full captain in the German Navy. He apologized for the sinking and then outlined the German justification—the fact that the *Zam*

Zam was running without lights, in radio silence
and operating under Admiralty direction. 'I am
sorry this had to happen,' said Captain Rogge. 'I
can only tell you that we shall do everything in
our power to put you safely ashore but you must
remember that this is war and in traveling on the
ocean you have assumed many risks! . . .' "

Mr. Murphy went on to describe how he and his
fellow passengers were transferred to the *Dresden*
which, after at least one narrow escape, reached St.-
Jean-de-Luz on the west coast of France after a run of
4,860 miles. Arrangements were eventually made for
him and the photographer Scherman to travel via Spain
and Portugal back to New York.

19

A NARROW ESCAPE

After getting our first and only stock of supplies
from the *Alsterufer* we steamed eastward to search
along the Capetown-Freetown route and the tanker
lanes between the West Indies oil refineries and Freetown. The *Alsterufer* had provided us with new aircraft,
food, ammunition and extra hands and above all with
mail—the first and only mail that we received throughout the whole mission. We also took on three new prize
officers. The first had been employed until recently in
the Berlin office of the Labor Front; he had not been to
sea for eight years and was a friendly old gentleman
who saw nothing wrong in appearing in the wardroom
in bedroom slippers, I sent him home—to our mutual
relief—in the *Dresden*. The second, having been blown
sky high by a mine during the invasion of Norway, had

been passed as only partially fit for duty—with the proviso that he should always keep his head protected from strong sunlight; it was obvious how useful he would be in the tropics—once again the Officers Appointments Bureau had excelled itself. The third man I kept; he was a good choice.

While on passage we began to transform the ship into the Dutch motorship *Brastagi;* we got as far as painting her upper works yellow but a heavy swell forced us to break off the work and it was not until June that the hull received its proper coat of light-gray paint which, as we had learned from our encounters with British ships, was less easy to see at night.

Although the aircraft maintenance crew had not received any instructions along with their new plane, they managed to assemble one of the *Arado 196s* sup-

Arado 196

plied by the *Alsterufer*. On May 1 it took off on its first flight to investigate a smoke cloud. The pilot reported that the smoke came from a ship steering south-east, but although we steamed at full speed until the afternoon, we still did not sight her and the plane had to take off to make a further search. From Bulla's next report it was clear that not only had the ship altered course, but that we were not fast enough to catch up with her. The new plane proved far more valuable than its predecessor, the *He 114*. Its chief advantage lay in its smaller size, which made it easier to handle over the side, and in its higher speed and shorter take-off.

On May 4 we met the *Babitonga*, disguised as the Dutch s.s. *Jaspara*; like the *Dresden* she had been despatched from Santos to act as our auxiliary. I sent her off to wait in position 30°S, 15°W. On May 13 we reached the Capetown-Freetown route, on which more than a year before we had claimed our first victim, the *Scientist*; she seemed to bring us luck for another ship came in sight quite close to where she had been sunk.

"She looks like a Dane of the Märsk class," I said. "Let's see if we can do without the guns. Signalman, make to her 'What ship? Do not use your wireless. Stop at once.'" The shutter of the signal lamp clacked out the message but nothing happened. "Wake him up with the searchlight," I ordered. "I don't want to shoot if I can help it."

But even the searchlight did not evoke a reply. After calling him up vainly for ten minutes I lost patience and ordered a round to be fired across his bows. The ship turned away at once and tried to escape, so I told Kasch to shoot up the wireless cabin. The very first salvo set the ship on fire and in half an hour she had sunk. We picked the survivors out of the water and steamed off at speed.

Our latest victim was not Danish, but British; she was the s.s. *Rabaul* of 5,618 tons, owned by the Carpenter Overseas Shipping Co., registered at Suva in Fiji, bound from England for the Cape with coal and piece goods. Our interrogation revealed the reason for the unusual casualness of her behavior. The officer of the watch was sixty-four years old; when disturbed by our challenge he had simply moved to the far end of the bridge on the assumption that "the other chap would eventually give up trying."

On May 17 we were standing along the inner-most of the courses which, according to a captured

English chart, were available to ships on passage between Capetown and Freetown. Following a habit we had acquired in the Indian Ocean, we had stopped engines and were drifting to save fuel. After the evening sing-song and the last rounds, a deep peace settled over the ship. The moon was very bright and visibility good. If anything turns up, I thought, we'll see it soon enough. And shortly after midnight we did!

The coxswain and a signalman reported it almost simultaneously. First one, then two humps appeared on the horizon, which grew into two large, blacked-out ships steaming in line ahead. I had been half asleep on the bridge deck and as soon as the message reached me, I sounded the alarm. The ships were heading straight toward us.

Any illusion that we had two big merchant ships in front of us quickly vanished. We were soon able to pick out the triangular silhouettes of warships, steaming in close order in line ahead at fourteen knots, between us and the moon. Fortunately the moon was shining right on us, making us more difficult to see; it is when the moon is behind you that it becomes dangerous. As we moved slowly ahead on the engines, being careful not to show any sparks, and gradually steered to starboard of the enemy, the silhouettes stood out even more clearly. One of them looked like an unusually powerful ship, the other loomed up as a giant rectangle—an aircraft carrier!

"That's no cruiser," I cried, "that's a *Nelson* class battleship!" I could clearly see the characteristic bows with the triple turrets. At that moment Commander Lorenzen arrived, rather out of breath, on the bridge. It was his job to make accurate notes of every order given in an action, for inclusion in the subsequent report. He had to wait a few seconds before his eyes grew accustomed to the dark, but as soon as he saw what was in front of us he realized what it signified.

"There are two of them, sir," he gasped in a horrified voice, "and isn't one of them a carrier?"

Despite the gravity of the situation, I could hardly keep from laughing and said, "Really, Lorenzen, you don't miss a thing, do you?"

Just then the voice pipe from the engine room croaked, "What's happening up on the bridge? There seem to be two ships out there. Aren't you going to attack them?"

"The two ships," said the officer of the watch, "are a battleship and a carrier." The questioner was left speechless.

The enemy came up so quickly that they must have seen us; if we had remained stopped they would have rammed us. But they altered course and passed astern of us; no one dared breathe during those seemingly endless minutes while we expected at every instant that they would alter course again and turn their searchlights on us—after which the end would come quickly. But nothing happened. The range was scarcely 7,000 yards and through our glasses we could see the battleship's bow wave. A single shell from her 16 inch guns would have blown us to atoms. We still did not dare to steam at full speed for fear of betraying our position by sparks; but very gradually we increased speed and turned slightly away, and at last the two ships disappeared over the horizon. I leaned over and spoke into the internal relay system.

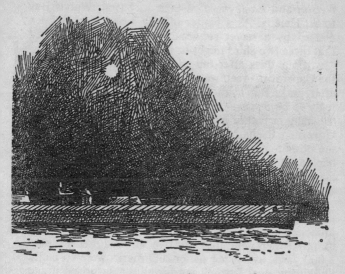

Nelson

"Attention all hands! Both enemy capital ships are now barely visible even through the best night glasses."

From somewhere in the darkness came the voice of the ship's wit, "Then they ought to use day glasses on the bridge so that they can see even less!" Our pent-up emotions found relief in a gale of laughter that swept through the ship.

We were still getting our breath back when a spout of flame suddenly shot up from the funnel. Some rust had got loose and caught fire, showering the whole ship with a rain of sparks. There was a yell of "Stop both engines!" but even so the sparks did not go out at once and, holding our breath once again, we looked alternately up at them and in the direction of the enemy. All was well.

Next morning—Sunday—the horizon was clear. I ordered "make and mend clothes" and held divine service, in which I offered up a special prayer of thanksgiving for our deliverance. We learned later that the

Nelson and *Eagle* were on their way from Walvis Bay to St. Helena. As a matter of fact, I had already been alerted by a secret service report, which had hinted that these two ships might be near Capetown.

Four days after our escape we sighted a ship on the Capetown-Freetown route and decided to attack her after dark. But at dusk she turned out rather surprisingly to be Swiss—the Greek *Master Elias Kulukundis* traveling in ballast from Lisbon to Madras under Swiss Government charter. I stopped her with a shot across the bows and sent the boarding party over to examine her cargo and English passengers. After making her master sign a promise not to use his wireless, we let the ship go.

A day or two later we sighted another ship and, as usual, kept out of sight until dusk. When we approached her, however, she also switched on her lights to prove her neutrality and we allowed her to pass 3,000 yards away; her nationality marks were so badly illuminated that I would not have been surprised if she had been torpedoed by one of our U-boats. An hour later we heard the ship calling Capetown and learned that she was the American *Charles H. Cramp.*

On May 24 we were delighted to see our seaplane waggling her wings as she returned from a patrol—this meant that she had sighted something. We shadowed the new target until nightfall and then stood in to attack. We scored hits with our very first salvo and soon the ship was in flames; her funnel was blown clear away from the ship and one mast broke in two, while fragments from her shattered bridge splashed into the water all around her. By the light of the flames we could see crates containing aircraft on her decks; the fire was so bright that I ordered her to be torpedoed, but we never seemed to have any luck with our torpedoes. The first one not only missed the target but circled around and nearly hit us instead; the second also developed some defect which took it in a wide arc away from the target, and it was only with the third that we managed to cause enough damage to sink the ship. She went down in nine minutes, leaving scores of survivors swimming in the water among overturned boats and pieces of wreckage.

She was the British s.s. *Trafalgar* of 4,530 tons belonging to the Glen Company of Glasgow, bound from England to Alexandria with coal and piece goods, including two aircraft. We picked up all her crew with the exception of twelve men who had gone down with her.

A signal from the Naval Staff which reached me at this time confirmed my suspicions about the danger of being D/F'd. Berlin had received proof that on May 5 no less than three British auxiliary cruisers, the *Queen of Bermuda, Alcantara* and *Asturias,* had been notified of a bearing obtained on three short signals of no more than eleven to fifteen letters. We also heard the sad news of the loss of the battleship *Bismarck;* a pall of gloom settled over the whole ship. Soon afterward we met the *Babitonga* again, handed over our prisoners and gave her a further rendezvous in the Central Atlantic. We spent some time overhauling engines and repairing ravages to the gray paint on our hull; then I steered to intercept shipping steaming westward out of Freetown.

In the second half of June we were due to meet the raider *Orion,* which was then operating in the southeastern sector of the Atlantic. By the middle of July the *Komet,* commanded by Admiral Eyssen, who had reached the Pacific via the Siberian route, was also due to operate in the South Atlantic. This number of ships seemed too large to me and I began to think once again of a plan to transfer my operational area to the Pacific. I had indeed considered returning home in September or October, but since both my ship and my men were perfectly fit, it seemed a pity to forego anything so advantageous. On June 16, 1941, *Atlantis* celebrated her 445th day at sea, thus breaking the record set up by the *Wolf* in the First World War; yet the thought of remaining at sea for a further six months was by no means unbearable. I decided to let this plan mature in my head a little longer and to talk it over with my officers.

A day or two later our seaplane sighted her fifth ship and we at once took up the chase. Just before dark we sank the British s.s. *Tottenham,* 4,640 tons, carrying valuable supplies for the British army in Palestine —aircraft, spare parts, uniforms, tractors and lorries. She was a new ship, built in 1940, with stump masts, a rounded bridge, and an armament which included a 4.7 inch gun and light and heavy AA guns with armored shields.

On June 22, when we were three hundred and thirty miles northeast of Trinidad, we made a dawn attack on yet another armed merchant ship. She started to use her wireless but our W/T office was able to jam her transmission with a fake signal addressed to Pernambuco which, sent out at full power, ran *"Hope to meet you next Friday love and kisses Evelyn."* The ship did her best to upset our gunners' aim, steaming at high speed and zigzagging wildly to avoid the fall of shot, all the time keeping her stern toward us to show the smallest target. We poured salvo after salvo after her; after the fortieth the forward guns stopped firing, as did No. 5 gun—they were overheated and would no longer run out, although our gunners tried to cool them down with sea water. We had to reduce our salvoes to one or two rounds at a time and I was on the point of abandoning the chase when the enemy suddenly— and much to our astonishment—stopped and lowered her boats. The master had handled his ship so cleverly that in one hundred and ninety-two rounds fired we had seen only one hit, though as it turned out she had in fact received four. She was the British s.s. *Balzac* of 5,372 tons, bound from Rangoon for Liverpool with a cargo of rice, bran, teak, wax and beans. After transferring some bags of mail from her, we sank her without further delay, picked up her survivors and destroyed their boats. This success brought our total to twenty-one ships of 139,591 tons and twenty-seven guns.

After spending a few days in an isolated position well away from all shipping routes, we shaped course on July 1 for a point three hundred miles north of Tristan da Cunha, where we were due to meet the raider *Orion,* commanded by Captain Weyher, on his return from the Indian Ocean. Weyher—like myself, a former captain of a sailing training ship—was a very angry man. For the last eight months he had been engaged in a completely fruitless search for enemy shipping. His ship was an oil-burning one with a high rate of consumption and as a result he was never free from anxiety about his endurance. He had never felt the same freedom as I had in the diesel-driven *Atlantis;* the *Orion* used more fuel in one week than we did in two months, and to cap everything he had incessant trouble with his engines.

He began at once to explain to me exactly why *Atlantis* would have to supply the *Orion* with a large quantity of fuel. As several of the *Orion*'s supply ships had failed to materialize in the last few days, we had in fact received instructions from the Naval Staff to supply her with sufficient fuel to reach home—about 700 tons—and I had worked out that we would be able to do this without compromising our plans for the Pacific. I told Weyher as much, but he was by no means prepared to agree. He wanted an extra 500 tons over and above this amount, which would enable him to operate without restriction until September and would give him a chance of making up for all his months of useless endeavor. I could not consent to this and he had to be satisfied with the 700 tons. We parted company on July 6, still good friends despite the difference of opinion over the fuel. The *Orion* sailed westward while we steered to the south, on the first leg of our journey to the Pacific.

20

CORAL STRANDS

At the beginning of our passage to the Pacific I gave a short talk to the crew in which I outlined my plans.

"After our successes of the last few months," I said, "we have almost a full load of fuel and food. There are enough stores on board to take us around the world several times without stopping. Now we are going into the Pacific, so our return home will be postponed for a few months. You may be disappointed by my decision and if you are, I cannot blame you. But try to understand the reasons which prompted me to take it and you will find it easier to cooperate with me."

On July 9 we caught a brief glimpse of Gough Island; for the third time we passed the Cape of Good Hope, but this time some nine hundred miles south of it. We had a regular escort of albatrosses, which glided without a wing beat in our lee; some of the men caught one once and found that its wing span measured over six feet. It staggered clumsily about the deck and was even seasick, but as soon as they put it over the side it took off in effortless flight. The Prince Edward Islands, followed by the islands of St. Paul and New Amsterdam, loomed above the horizon and then dropped astern of us. We sighted no ships. The weather was just as might be expected in the Roaring Forties; after we had passed the Cape the prevailing wind blew up to force 11 and once again *Atlantis* displayed her fine seagoing qualities.

By the time we reached the longitude of the Kerguelens, we had tried more than a hundred times to send a short signal home, but without success; the only one acknowledged by Berlin was the signal in which we reported having left the Indian Ocean. The enemy must have taken bearings on these transmissions because after a few days the British Admiralty reported rather vaguely that there was a "German ship in the Kerguelen area."

The duties of our radio operators were not limited to wireless routines; they were also responsible for all musical and artistic entertainment on board. Gramophone concerts, bulletins of news from the world's press and the issue of the "ship's newspaper" were some of the methods with which they sought to enliven the tedium of our voyage. Strangely enough, the most popular among our library of two hundred and fifty records were by no means those of the light music so much beloved by Germans on shore. We never gave any patriotic talks of the type broadcast at home; my officers produced carefully prepared lectures on the political situation in Australia or the United States, while other speakers told of their experiences in Siberia and one of the *Graf Spee* survivors told of his escape from La Plata via La Paz, which ended on board *Atlantis*. Their listeners were grateful for anything to distract them.

We had celebrated our 500th day at sea off the Crozet Islands; now New Zealand was astern of us and Auckland Island was just visible on the horizon. Seven weeks after parting company with the *Orion* we were once more in waters where we might hope to find some enemy ships. Two hours after sunset on September 10, when we were well eastward of the Kermadec Islands, we came upon a poorly darkened ship steaming toward us. We could see at once that she was a merchant ship and promptly unmasked our guns as we swung around to follow her. As usual we were ready to jam her transmissions, but when we heard her "QQQ" signal and my radio operators hastened to blot it out, nothing happened. In his hurry one of them had made a false connection and so the ship was allowed to signal undisturbed. She gave her name as *Silvaplana* and followed this with her position. I signaled her by light. *"Stop at once. Do not use your wireless,"* and she promptly did as she was told. We were able to drop our flaps again without firing the guns.

The *Silvaplana,* of 4,793 tons, was a modern Norwegian motorship belonging to the Tschudi & Eitzen Company; she was an important capture for in her holds were quantities of sago, crude rubber, hides and spices which she was bringing from Singapore to New York. I decided to retain her in company until we could replenish her with the oil we had been promised from Japan, and then send her back to France. Our hopes that her SOS had not been picked up soon faded when several Australian shore stations began to repeat it. We at once cancelled the SOS and this was acknowledged and relayed by Rartonga and other stations, but we did not seem to have allayed their suspicions entirely; twelve hours later the *Silvaplana* was told to repeat her cancellation in code, but this of course she could not do. We parted company with her after arranging to meet again in four days time some four hundred miles south of Tubuai Island. Here we very laboriously transferred one hundred and twenty tons of rubber by boat from the *Silvaplana*'s cargo as ballast for *Atlantis;* we then despatched the *Silvaplana* to await orders off the Orne Bank. We ourselves were due to meet the supply ship *Münsterland* coming from Japan. It was better to keep our prize at a distance rather than to run the risk of assembling too many ships in one place, as one of the *Komet*'s prizes, the *Kota Nopan,* was also due at the rendezvous. We were surprised to find the *Komet* herself there as well; the *Münsterland* had been held up by a typhoon and arrived two days late.

"The *Komet*'s commander is an admiral, sir," Mohr reminded me as we came up to the other ships. "As a flag officer he has the right to be received with full ceremony."

"You're quite right, Mohr," I said. "See to it, please."

Shortly afterward our guns roared a salute to the admiral—probably the first and only salute ever fired in a German admiral's honor in the Pacific. When Rear Admiral Eyssen came on board *Atlantis,* my crew were fallen in on deck and he was piped over the side.

Our preliminary conferences were conducted in a very friendly atmosphere, but difficulties set in with the arrival of Captain Uebel in the *Münsterland;* the *Komet*'s commander wanted to take over part of the fresh food she had brought for *Atlantis.*

"*Komet,*" he said, "has only been restored once—from the *Anneliese Essberger*—and then inadequately. I must insist on having a share of the *Münsterland*'s stores."

The only solution was to work out mutually how often each ship had received a proper ration of vitamins and how long she had been without them. Results showed that *Atlantis* had not had any fresh vegetables for the past 540 days, whereas the *Komet* had been restocked on at least five occasions. Once the supply of potatoes brought from Germany had been exhausted, we had had potatoes served at only thirty-five meals, the last one being four months previously; while the *Komet* had had them at fifty-seven meals, the last one three days ago. Confronted with this overwhelming evidence in our favor, the *Komet*'s commander had to give way; he did so with a good grace, asking only to be given some of our beer.

We remained four days in company with the *Komet,* the *Kota Nopan* and the *Münsterland.* The crew of the *Komet* had a lot to tell us. Their ship had begun the breakthrough under escort from some Russian icebreakers but without warning they abandoned her to her own devices and she had to make her way alone along the coast of Siberia through fields of pack ice and icebergs to the Bering Sea—a remarkable feat of seamanship.

The transfer of supplies and fuel between the ships went forward as planned, though somewhat hampered by bad weather. In the *Münsterland* we encountered for the first time a supply ship that had been stocked by an expert. Nothing had been forgotten. The Naval Attaché in Tokyo, Vice Admiral Wenneker, had commanded a big ship in the Atlantic at the beginning of the war and we benefited now from his personal experience.

Atlantis had now been at sea for exactly eighteen

months—six months longer than had been originally planned. With full storerooms and bunkers she was theoretically capable of remaining at sea for another year—until the end of 1942. But from a practical point of view the state of her engines and the moral and physical demands upon her crew set such definite limits to her endurance that I decided to terminate my mission at the end of 1941. We would then have been at sea for twenty-one months and have fulfilled all our tasks; moreover the long December nights were the most favorable for our return to Germany. The program I laid down was as follows: operations in the Pacific until October 19; move to the South Atlantic; spend eight or ten days there overhauling engines, allowing ten more days for operations; then return home, where I reckoned to arrive in the new moon period of December 20.

Christmas at home! The idea seemed almost incredible. But it was not Christmas yet and it is usually the unexpected that happens at sea.

The American press had seized with avidity upon the subject of auxiliary cruisers. There were whole columns about "raiders," "pirates," "rattlesnakes of the sea" and "Nazi plans to destroy the freedom of the seas." The radio broadcasts were as full of it as the newspapers; they finally reached the point where, to our amusement, they claimed that no less than thirteen German raiders had been destroyed in the Pacific.

Mohr had found a chart on board the *Silvaplana* that showed the course followed by the ship on her last voyage through the Pacific. We steamed along this and then cruised across the narrow shipping lanes off the Tuamotu Archipelago, using the plane whenever possible, but day succeeded day without a sign of a smoke cloud. At last I decided to come under the lee of one of the islands where, sheltered from the heavy swell, we could launch the plane more frequently and thus enlarge our radius of search. Tuamotu means "low islands"; they "are a swarm of countless small coral atolls, stretching over hundreds of square miles right across the equator." The very thought of a "coral atoll" appealed to our imagination and the crew's excitement turned to delight when I announced that we were going to visit one of them. The one I chose was called Vana Vana; I selected it not so much for its pretty name—which conjured up visions of bronzed maidens clad in nothing but a hair comb and a flower behind their ears—as because the sailing directions indicated that it was not inhabited by missionaries or any large native settlement.

Vana Vana is a circular atoll studded with coconut palms and surrounded by thundering surf, beyond which lies a bright-hued beach and a lagoon of magical blue. I brought the ship in as close as I could at slow speed; there was plenty of water beneath her, as the bottom fell away steeply within fifty yards of the beach. We spent forty-eight hours at Vana Vana, sending the plane out on patrol three times a day, but without result. Meanwhile we managed to get nearly every man of the crew on shore—the first land they had trodden in ten months—and they returned laden with fresh coconuts which made a welcome change to our diet.

From there we moved to Pitcairn Island, still flying off the plane at regular intervals but without success. I found a safe and sheltered anchorage in the lee of Henderson Island, one hundred miles NE of Pitcairn, and once again I could allow the crew to land. But Henderson is not an atoll—it is of volcanic origin, rocky and thickly covered with primitive vegetation. It is about three miles in circumference but the thickly matted undergrowth made it almost impossible to move about; there were no animals and even insects were lacking. There were a few palm trees on the beach, grown from nuts washed up by the sea, and close by, some of the men found a board with the inscription, "This island belongs to King George the Fifth." From the rest of the writing, now almost illegible, they made out that a British cruiser had been there years before and had left this board behind to remove any doubts about the ownership of the island. After a few more days of vain search, we shaped course for Cape Horn.

While on passage to Cape Horn we heard of the loss of the supply ship serving the U-boats off Capetown and I promptly offered the services of *Atlantis* for the purpose. On October 29 we rounded the famous Cape in a calm sea but heavy snow squalls; the water was at freezing point but we did not see any icebergs. For a time I considered making an attack on the whaling ships stationed in South Georgia, but I eventually abandoned the idea, partly because I had no charts of these little-known waters and partly because I was under orders from the Naval Staff to rendezvous with *U 68*. A few days later we met the U-boat and steamed off together to a position decided upon between ourselves; I was anxious to safeguard against any breach of cipher security and the last thing I wanted was to be surprised while refueling the U-boat. I had heard of several occasions when a meeting between U-boats had been interrupted, but this had never happened when surface ships met.

The commanding officer of the U-boat, Commander Merten, was an old friend of mine from pre-war days. We had sailed in many a regatta together and had represented the German Navy both at home and abroad. It was good to see him again and we sat down for a drink in the main saloon, where my officers and I had discussed so many plans and entertained so many defeated enemies.

"After refueling your boat," I told him, "I had intended to overhaul my engines and then go on patrol for a few days. But now I have been ordered to refuel *U 162*."

"I know," said Merten, "that's Bauer's boat. I read the signal."

"That may be very desirable in the interests of the war, you know," I went on, "but it is very inconvenient for me and in any case I don't see the need for it. The supply ship *Python* is shortly due to cross the equator on her way to her area off St. Helena. Bauer could have refueled just as well from her."

Two days later Merten left us and after doing some repairs to the main engines, we resumed our search to the west. Within forty-eight hours Bulla had reported a ship but she turned out to be a neutral; he sighted another the next day but she was too fast for us and we had to abandon the chase. On landing, the plane sustained damage to her supercharger; this was a minor matter but it meant that the engine would have to be replaced, and this took so long that she was out of service for twenty-four hours. For the next five days the trade wind blew so hard that she could not take off at all. When at length the wind eased she got into the air, but on landing set down so clumsily that she swamped one of her floats and capsized. The crew were rescued and the plane was salved but she was so badly damaged that there was no chance of her being able, as I had hoped, to take off the following day, when we were due to meet *U 126*.

The rendezvous position with *U 126*, known as *Lily 10*, lay three hundred and fifty miles northwest of Ascension Island. And there, in the early morning of November 22, 1941, the U-boat came in sight as scheduled.

PART FOUR

HOMEWARD BOUND

November 22nd, 1941–New Year's Day, 1942

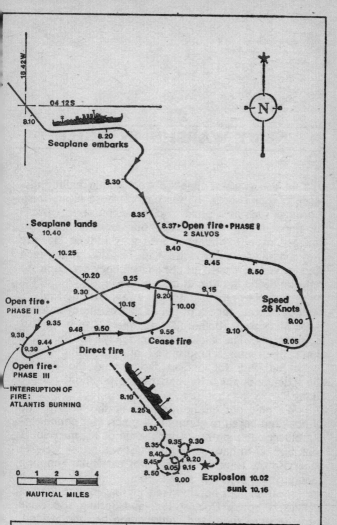

The sinking of the Raider ATLANTIS,
by the British Cruiser Devonshire * * *
November 22 1941

21

ENEMY WARSHIP IN SIGHT!

In a very short time we were within hailing distance of the U-boat. It was one of those clear, fresh mornings such as we had so often encountered. *Atlantis* stopped and we launched our motorboat, which chugged over to where the long gray U-boat lay, her low conning tower crowded with bearded young men who waved across to us. My chief engineer came to report a defect in our port engine.

"Better to repair it straight away, sir," he said. "I shall have to change a piston in one of the cylinders."

"Very well, Kielhorn," I answered, "so be it, if it is necessary. The sooner you're ready, the better. I don't like lying semi-disabled at a meeting point; compared with the Indian Ocean and the Pacific, the Atlantic is much too narrow and populous for my liking."

We paid out the hose pipe over the stern to the U-boat and began to pump oil into her. Her commanding officer came on board with some of his men and I took him off to have some breakfast while they went to supervise the transfer of their own particular supplies. Lieutenant Bauer had sailed from France only a few weeks earlier and he answered my eager questions as well as he could. Doctors Reil and Sprung also came into the ward room and conversation became general. Mohr, my adjutant, was still asleep in his bunk; he told me afterward how he was being troubled by a dream—the same one that he had had regularly for the past six months. In this dream he saw an enemy cruiser bearing 20 degrees to port; and he knew that this spelt the end of the raider—loss, injury, perhaps death, for an auxiliary cruiser is not an armored ship and a real warship is much faster and more powerful.

At sixteen minutes past eight there came a yell from one of the lookouts: "Three-funneled ship bearing red two-oh!"

The alarm bells went off almost at the same moment and within seconds we cast off lines over the stern and the hose pipe connecting us with the U-boat had been capped. I ordered full speed ahead and called down the voice pipe to the chief engineer to tell him to get the port engine running as quickly as he could. We turned hard a-port to show our stern to the enemy and also to hide the U-boat. It was a cruiser that was chasing us and I had quickly recognized her class for I had been first lieutenant of the cruiser *Karlsruhe* in 1936 when she had been berthed alongside the three-funneled HMS *Dorsetshire* in Hong Kong. This cruiser

Launching Walrus

was identical to her and she was close enough now for us to see her launch her aircraft by catapult.

The only boat we had in the water was lying alongside *U 126* so there was no time for Bauer and his men to get back on board their U-boat. His first lieutenant took over command and dived as soon as the lines were clear, leaving Bauer cursing his luck on the deck of *Atlantis*. We watched the aircraft anxiously as it flew in a wide circle around us. Even if the pilot had not sighted the U-boat he must have seen the telltale hose pipe, lying in a pool of oil between us. Sure enough one of my lookouts reported as calmly as he could, "Aircraft is signaling *SSS*." We all knew what those letters stood for—*Submarine*.

The enemy cruiser kept carefully outside the range of our guns, steaming back and forth along the horizon. Then came a flash and a salvo of warning shots howled over our heads.

"Eight inch guns!" said someone near me. Another man muttered, "Yes, it's better to give than to receive . . ." We turned south-southwest, followed by the motorboat; the hose pipe already lay some distance astern. As the aircraft continued to circle us some of my crew waved to it in a pretence of friendliness for I was still intent on gaining time and keeping up the disguise. There was no hope of fighting back; our only chance lay in luring the enemy across the U-boat's torpedo tubes.

For a moment I wondered whether it was pure chance that had brought the cruiser down upon us at such an inopportune moment; or had we been betrayed in some way? But there was no time for reflection. The cruiser's guns flashed twice and two lofty columns of water towered out of the sea astern of us.

"Stop engines," I ordered. "Hard a-port. Let him see that we are hove-to."

There was no point in trying to escape; the best we could do on one engine was ten knots, while the cruiser could shell us to pieces without ever coming within range of our guns. I ordered the "Am stopped" signal to be hoisted and at the same time the W/T office began to transmit a prearranged signal, *"RRR Polyphemus . . ."* followed by our position. I was still trying to bring the cruiser within range of *U 126*'s torpedoes.

First the plane and then the cruiser began to signal by light *"N—N—I"* followed by *"What ship?"*

"What shall I reply, sir?" asked the signalman on the bridge.

"Acknowledge slowly and ask him to repeat," I said. The signalman grasped my meaning and for nearly an hour he continued to exchange signals with the cruiser, repeating the name *Polyphemus* and asking *"What do you want now?"* Every moment that we could gain in this way might bring us nearer to salvation through the U-boat's torpedoes.

I did not know at the time that after diving, *U 126* had remained close to us on the assumption that the cruiser would come in close to engage us and thus give him a chance to attack. I was equally unaware that Bauer's first lieutenant had mistaken the enemy's first salvo for aircraft bombs aimed at him and had accordingly taken the boat down to three hundred feet; he had thus been unable to use his periscope to get a clear picture of the situation.

After steaming up and down for some time, the cruiser opened fire on us from nearly ten miles away. The first salvo was short, but the second straddled us and a splinter struck the foredeck. I turned hard a-starboard and made smoke but before the ship could answer her helm a third salvo hit us. One shell exploded in the aircraft hangar, knocked out part of our electricity supply and set fire to the seaplane.

Then things began to happen quickly. All the internal telephones failed and it became difficult to pass orders. Even when we had switched over to the auxiliary supply, the current came through so irregularly that we could not send the prearranged signal to the Naval Staff. The boats had to be lowered from the davits by hand and our attempts to extinguish the fire in the hangar were of no avail. Soon we had to abandon the fore bridge. Then the wheel and the engine-room telegraphs went dead and messages for helm and engines had to be passed by a chain of men.

A respite came when our smoke began to take effect. It upset the enemy's shooting and thereafter we sustained comparatively few hits. We stopped immediately behind the smoke screen, and the enemy's shells fell well beyond us.

Nevertheless there was no hope of escape: my one concern was to save the lives of as many of the crew as possible and to get all the boats launched before scuttling the ship. Some of the boats had already been damaged by splinters and there was no time to lose. The cruiser had by now maneuvered clear of the smoke and was firing repeatedly at ten miles range. But we had time to get all the boats and rafts into the water and we even hoisted out two cutters that were not slung from davits. *Atlantis* had sustained eight direct hits, but our casualties were remarkably few. When nearly all the crew had gone over the side, I ordered Lieutenant Fehler to scuttle her. Alas! just before we abandoned ship, two men were killed and the first lieutenant was wounded; shells were bursting inboard and hurling splinters through the ship's side.

At last, all the boats were away; the scuttling charges went off in the engine room; *Atlantis* listed to port and began to sink stern first. Apart from myself, the only men left on board were Mohr, the chief coxswain and a group of men acting under Fehler's orders. Thoughts raced through my head like a film that has been speeded up. Had I done all that I could? Was there no alternative? How could I save as many men as possible and what damage could I inflict on the enemy? Could I—would I—return home without my ship? Would I not rather do the other thing . . . ? And again I found myself hoping that the U-boat would still be able to bring off an attack. But time was running out: fresh decisions had to be made every second. Just as the last scuttling charge went off, the ready-use ammunition forward got a direct hit and blew up. I was alone on the bridge as Mohr was destroying the secret papers.

Chief Coxswain Pigors came up saying, "It's time to leave, sir." I shook my head silently. "At least let us keep on the side away from the firing," he insisted. We went to the other side of the W/T office. It was difficult to hear each other above the crackling of the flames and the explosion of the shells. I still could not make up my mind to leave the ship, but Pigors was insistent.

"There's no sense in staying here, sir," he yelled in my ear. "There's nothing more you can do, but the men out there need you!"

I shook my head again. "Please leave me, Pigors . . ."

"No!" he bawled again, "this is our last chance and if you don't come with me, sir, I'll stay here too."

That settled it. We left the bridge.

Mohr, Fehler and his men were already swarming down the falls or jumping overboard. Pigors and I were the last to jump and we had to swim hard to get clear of the sinking ship. The enemy was still pouring shells into her and two men were killed as they swam— if the enemy had been using nose fuses instead of base fuses our casualties would have been still heavier, as there were more than one hundred men in the water. Five or six more salvoes came over and then the secondary magazine went up in a sheet of flame. The boat deck was already touching the water. Suddenly a man appeared on the forecastle. He had received no answer over the telephone and had remained at his post between decks. He had only come on deck because the ship seemed to be behaving so oddly. When he saw what was happening he hesitated no longer and jumped for his life.

Atlantis sank by the stern at about 10 A.M. in position 4°20′S, 18°35′W. She flew no flag, for I had kept up the disguise until the last; I did not want the enemy to know which ship they had sunk so that they would continue to search for us. The men in the water gave three cheers for their ship. The enemy plane flew over us again, but the cruiser had already disappeared, having presumably steamed off as soon as *Atlantis* went down.

Mohr later wrote this description of the scene that followed.

"The boat that I eventually got into was terribly overcrowded. There were sixty of us squatting on our haunches. On looking around I was glad to see so many trusted friends near me. In my boat sat the chief coxswain, who had stayed to the last with the captain on the bridge and who now held the tiller. We had not yet thought about getting out the oars. The weather was unusually calm. The sun was shining through a slight haze and there was almost no wind. Our boat was rising and falling on a long swell and as it lifted us up we could see the other boats a few hundred yards away, also drifting without rowing. We were on the fringe of a mass of wreckage that marked the spot where the ship had gone down and objects that we recognized were floating all around us. 'What's that?' asked someone and another replied, 'It must be the port awning stanchion.' Someone else recognized the starboard bridge companion and then suddenly Lieutenant Bulla called out, 'There's my chest of drawers!' It was floating toward us and Bulla took out all the things he thought he might need —handkerchiefs and his beloved Dunhill pipe. Then it floated away again.

"Where was the *Dorsetshire?* After her aircraft had flown over us once more at low altitude we had no thought about her. We searched the horizon but there was nothing to be seen. Then we heard the bosun's call and we saw our captain standing up in one of the boats. He called out, 'All boats gather around me!' We roused ourselves, got out the oars and began to pull. Soon all the boats were assembled around the captain's cutter; there were four big steel cutters, three motorboats and five collapsible dinghies. The captain's voice brought us back to reality. We were all rather stunned by what had happened, for we had always believed in our own good fortune. But there were some tremendous problems to be solved if we wanted to return home alive. . . ."

We got together all the men who were still swimming and built some rafts out of the wreckage floating around us. There were sharks everywhere but they only went for the dead and did not attempt to touch the living. We picked up the last of the swimmers at about noon and soon afterward the U-boat appeared; she reembarked her own commanding officer and took on board all the wounded and the men on rafts. Then she took in tow an empty cutter that had come to the surface after *Atlantis* had sunk, as well as the motorboat from the *Teddy,* which had been launched before the cruiser had appeared and had since been swamped.

As soon as we were all assembled I called the roll and established that seven men were missing. Besides the wounded, *U 126* also embarked all those specialists from the ship's company who would be of the greatest value at home—ten officers, six CPOs, sixteen petty officers and twenty-three ratings. The rest of the men were distributed among the two motorboats and the four steel cutters, each commanded by an officer. To avoid overloading the boats during the long tow, we put fifty-two men in lifejackets on the U-boat's deck, with orders to jump overboard and join one or other of the boats in the event of the U-boat having to dive.

Our voyage began at 4:00 P.M. on November 22. Until such time as we received orders from the Naval Staff, our destination would be the coast of Brazil. The fine weather and a following sea helped us to maintain a speed of six to seven knots under tow, but we had to stop fairly often to mend the tow lines. The yawing of the heavy motorboats put a heavy strain on the ropes, while the boats themselves kept filling with water through planks that had started. At noon on November 23 by dead reckoning we had covered one hundred and fifty of the nine hundred and fifty miles to Pernambuco. If the weather held we could reckon to cover the remaining eight hundred miles in five or six days. Our principal worry was the supply of tow lines, as the U-boat only carried a limited number and they were fast running out.

To the men in the open boats it already seemed

that they had spent a lifetime in them. The boats shipped water so frequently that it was soon up to the level of the thwarts where they sat shivering. By day the sun shone pitilessly down on their heads and the nights were so icy cold that they huddled together for warmth. They lived on ship's biscuit and water, the iron rations carried in each boat. Later on, the U-boat was able to help them out.

Toward evening on the second day we received the welcome news that the Naval Staff had ordered three U-boats and the *Python* to steam to our aid. It is difficult to describe our feelings of relief. We sighted the supply ship next morning. Never has any ship received so warm a welcome and an hour later we were waving our thanks to the U-boat from the deck of our new home, as the *Python* hoisted in our boats.

We fell like wolves on our first real meal. It tasted marvelous and we washed it down with brandy and coffee. Then our comrades shared out their clothing among us and put down mattresses in the hold where the men could stretch themselves out after sitting so long in a cramped position. The *Python* had been a liner belonging to the African Fruit Company of Hamburg and by a curious chance I had traveled in her to England for the Coronation in 1937. I was now given the same cabin as on my first trip in her.

U 126 completed her refueling on November 24 and at dusk she sailed away, carrying with her our heartfelt good wishes. This was the first night of real security for us survivors of *Atlantis,* and in the next few days we were able to make a calm appraisal of recent events. Soon afterward however our morale suffered a relapse and we began to wonder whether everything had been done to prevent the destruction of our ship. On November 25 I wrote the last entry in the raider's war diary as follows:

"After successfully carrying out her mission and covering 102,000 miles in 622 days at sea, *Atlantis* was located and destroyed when on the point of returning home and while engaged upon a supply operation which was not included in her operational orders. Our bitterness at the loss of our ship has been intensified by the thought that we had to abandon her without a fight ... I wish to emphasize that throughout our mission my ship's company have carried out their duties cheerfully and efficiently. They have shown what German seamen can do even under the most trying circumstances."

But brave words alone could not exclude the bitterness of my thoughts at this time. An endless series of questions, mostly unanswerable, kept running through my head. Why did my willingness to help Merten with supplies have to lead to the second supply operation with *U 126*? And why at that spot? Why had I not followed my usual habit of steaming in company with the U-boat for two hundred miles to guard against surprise? The fact that the port engine was defective was no excuse, for I could have steamed on the starboard engine alone. Even so, would we have escaped detection by the British cruiser's plane? It was, as I say, impossible to answer these questions, but it was equally impossible to suppress them. Could there be any question of treachery? How otherwise explain the arrival of the cruiser at the exact time and place of our meeting with the U-boat? Why should she have launched her plane as soon as she sighted us? She must have assumed at first that *Atlantis* was a merchant ship. I wondered if we would ever solve the riddle.

I was afforded some measure of consolation by a signal from Grand Admiral Raeder which read: "*I approve your decision to save your crew and maintain your disguise by scuttling your ship when you had no chance of offering resistance.*" In another signal received on the same day the *Python* was ordered to replenish *U 68* (Commander Merten) and *UA* (Commander Eckermann) on November 30 and *U 124* (Lieutenant Jochen Mohr) and *U 129* (Lieutenant Nico Clausen) on December 4 at a meeting point off the coast of Southwest Africa. Thereafter she was to return home with the survivors of *Atlantis*.

The *Python* met *U 68* on the evening of November 30 in position 27°53'S, 3°55'W, some seven hundred miles south of St. Helena. Barely two weeks had elapsed since Merten had been my welcome guest aboard *Atlantis* and now we met again—I as a survivor on a strange ship while he had behind him a successful mission to Walvis Bay and Capetown. *UA* did not arrive until dawn the following morning, thus causing a delay which was to have disastrous consequences. The *Python*'s lookouts had been reinforced by experienced ratings from *Atlantis,* but the *Python*'s commanding officer did not think it necessary to station a man, as I would have done, at the masthead. The weather forecast was uncertain so it was decided not to move the ships further to the north, as bad weather might prevent the transfer of torpedoes.

At 3:30 P.M. on the 1st, just as *U 68* was starting to take on food supplies, one of my lookouts reported a three-funneled ship approaching slowly at about nineteen miles range; she was promptly identified as a cruiser. The man in the crows-next—six feet above my lookout—had sighted nothing.

Supply operations were broken off at once, lines were hauled in and the rubber dinghies and fuel pipes cast off. The *Python* worked up to emergency speed and steered northeast. The sudden call for high revolutions caused her to emit a large puff of black smoke which must have drawn the enemy's attention to her, for the cruiser suddenly altered course and steamed after us at high speed. It would have been better if the *Python* had started off at a slower speed to avoid making so much smoke, but her commander could not be blamed for this as he was quite inexperienced in those tactics of war with which we had become so familiar. We were able to identify our attacker as a cruiser of the *London* class.

Both U-boats dived as quickly as they could, but when the alarm was given, *U 68* was in the middle of embarking the last torpedo and was lying with hatch covers upon. *UA* only needed to cast off the hose pipes. The *Python*'s "skimmer" could not be hoisted inboard and was left behind. The cruiser passed it, giving it a wide berth, about half an hour later. Although the *Python*'s commander correctly drew his assailant across the path of the two U-boats, *UA* was the only one to get into a firing position. *U 68* crashdived before being properly trimmed and started to go down like a stone; by the time she had been brought under control the enemy cruiser was so far away that Merten could only send a curse after her. *UA* fired five torpedoes in two salvoes from 3,000 yards range but her captain had underestimated the speed of the target and all torpedoes missed.

From then on things happened just as we had expected. The cruiser rapidly overtook us and fired a warning salvo from eleven miles away, whereupon the *Python* turned away and stopped. By mistake the after smoke-making apparatus was then turned on, but fortunately the cruiser did not reopen fire. We had plenty of time to lower the boats and to throw into them the supplies of food still lying on the deck, which had been set ready for the U-boats. The motorboats took the rubber dinghies in tow and the whole chain of boats moved away from the ship to get out of the line of fire, as we expected the shooting to begin at any moment. The only people left on board were Lieutenant Commander (S) Lueders, commanding the *Python,* the scuttling party and Lieutenant Fehler.

Before abandoning ship, the *Atlantis* survivors went to the storekeeper to get some warm clothing. True to his profession, however, he refused to issue any clothing without getting a receipt properly made out for it. Eventually he was put into one of the boats and the men got their jackets and trousers without a receipt.

The bridge of the *Python* had already started to burn when the scuttling charges went off at 6:40 P.M. The engine room was soon in flames as well: we had made our preparations carefully and had sprinkled petrol everywhere to help the fire. After forty minutes the *Python* listed over to port and sank. The cruiser disappeared toward the south. Both U-boats appeared shortly before sunset but they had to dive again be-

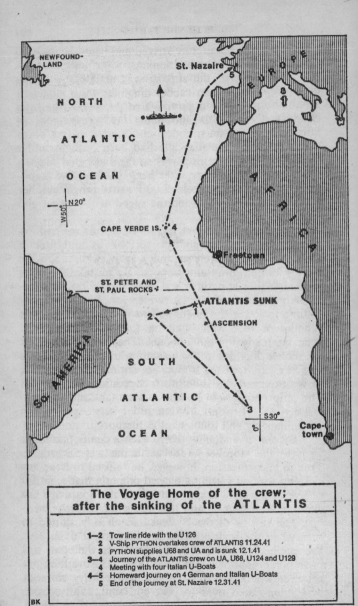

The Voyage Home of the crew;
after the sinking of the ATLANTIS

1—2	Tow line ride with the U126
2	V-Ship PYTHON overtakes crew of ATLANTIS 11.24.41
3	PYTHON supplies U68 and UA and is sunk 12.1.41
3—4	Journey of the ATLANTIS crew on UA, U68, U124 and U129
4	Meeting with four Italian U-Boats
4—5	Homeward journey on 4 German and Italian U-Boats
5	End of the journey at St. Nazaire 12.31.41

cause the cruiser's aircraft arrived and flew low over the spot where the *Python* had sunk.

The scene of the sinking was marked by eleven ship's boats and seven rubber dinghies. They held four hundred and fourteen survivors of the *Python* and the *Atlantis*. Between us and home lay 5,000 miles of enemy-infested waters.

22

"HOME IS THE SAILOR . . ."

HMS *Dorsetshire*'s plane disappeared and the two U-boat captains, Eckermann and Merten, were confronted with the task of getting us all safely home to the nearest friendly port, a quarter of the earth's circumference away. At first Eckermann insisted on assuming command of the entire expedition. He said he was "the senior officer present in command of an operational ship." However Merten and I between us managed to convince him of the inappropriateness of thinking in terms of seniority in such a position, and as Merten had taken me on board his boat, *U 68* became the "senior ship."

Each U-boat then embarked one hundred men below deck. The remainder were distributed equally between the lifeboats and the dinghies, which were hoisted on to the U-boats' decks. Each U-boat had to take five lifeboats in tow, leaving the motor "skimmer" to proceed under its own power and keep the boats under tow supplied with food and drink. During the next few days this little boat, which had always suffered from a defective engine, moved continuously from one lifeboat to the next without ever stopping or breaking down, followed everywhere by the eyes of the men who sat in the boats, parched with thirst and panting in the heat of the equatorial sun.

Long after dark on December 1, 1941, the two U-boats started off with their tows on course northwest, and the flag officer, U-boats, was informed by signal.

How thankful I was that I had ordered *Atlantis*'s boats to be hoisted on board the *Python* and kept ready for immediate use, despite the space they took up on deck. They were now fully provisioned—which was just as well, as the reprovisioning of *U 68* had had to be broken off at an early stage.

When we began our journey two other U-boats —Lieutenant Jochen Mohr's *U 124* and Lieutenant Nico Clausen's *U 129*—were some four hundred to six hundred miles to the north. On the night of December 2 both U-boats received orders from the flag officer, U-boats, to steam with all despatch toward *UA* and *U 68* and each take over one-quarter of the survivors.

By now we had instituted a proper routine. One-third of the survivors were below deck, one-third sat in the dinghies on deck with lifejackets on, and one-third were in the lifeboats. When the time to change came around, the men in the lifeboats went on the upper deck of the U-boats, those who had been on the upper deck went below and those who had been below got into the lifeboats. If the U-boats had to dive, the lifeboats would be cast off, the dinghies would be floated and the men below would take part in the diving operations. We rehearsed this every morning.

At noon on December 2 Eckermann reported our position and at the same time asked *U 124* and *U 129* to keep permanent W/T watch on the "Africa" wavelength, which was used by all U-boats operating in the South Atlantic. *U 129* reached us on the afternoon of December 3 and took off Captain Lueders and the whole of the *Python*'s crew with the exception of three men. As *U 124* was not yet in contact with us and *U 129* was rather short of fuel, I decided to keep the latter with us for the time being.

On the afternoon of December 2 *U 68* had sighted a tanker but although Merten was itching to attack, he resisted the impulse in favor of safeguarding his passengers. Not so Eckermann. Having sighted a merchant ship on December 3 he cast off his tow lines, launched his dinghies and despite my remonstrances went off in pursuit. His chase was unsuccessful.

The greater part of the crew spent a whole week in those open boats. Hardly one of them had more than a shirt to cover his body and even fewer had anything warm to wear at night, when the temperature dropped almost to freezing point. By day the sun shone pitilessly down upon them, blinding eyes that were already inflamed with salt. The boats were crammed so full that nobody could move; the men just sat there in a sleepless coma, tossed back and forth by the unending swell. It was only rarely that the U-boats could send hot food over to the lifeboats; every minute of fine weather was precious and the frayed tow lines were constantly breaking. And when this happened they had to be laboriously salved and passed to the boat ahead.

With the return of *UA* and the arrival of *U 129* I decided to scuttle the smaller boats from the *Python* and *Atlantis*. From here on, *U 68* and *UA* each took one of the big steel cutters in tow, while the "skimmer" continued under its own power. We had still heard nothing from Jochen Mohr except for one signal to flag officer, U-boats, in which he reported the sinking of a British light cruiser (the *Dunedin*); the position he gave showed that he was on his way toward us. I was very worried about this lack of cooperation and decided that if necessary I would try to continue the operation with the three U-boats only; the constant transmission of radio beacon signals which remained unanswered was getting on my nerves. It would be so easy for the enemy to locate us through our own transmissions and to send a force to destroy us.

By December 4 *U 124* had still not come in sight. *UA* signaled our position once again, albeit with an error of thirty miles, and began to send out continuous beacon signals. The position was now so confused that *U 68* entered the fray on her own account and asked *U 124* to report her position on the "Africa" wavelength. An hour later *UA* again asked *U 124* to watch for beacon signals, report her own position and then wait for a correction of our position, but *U 124* made no reply.

I wrote in my diary at this time: "The position is becoming very unsatisfactory. We cannot steam at more than six or seven knots in the best conditions, and we are now using up fuel and food without making any corresponding progress. There is always the possibility that the fine weather we have had so far will change and we shall no longer be able to tow. As *U 124* has made no report, her loss must be reckoned with. I am therefore preparing to embark in the U-boats those men who are still in the lifeboats."

In consultation with Merten, I decided to reduce our general speed; we had already reached the spot where the British cruiser had been sunk and if *U 124* were still afloat, she certainly would not be any further to the north of us. It seemed probable that she had steamed past us owing to *UA*'s inaccurate position report. In the evening we were surprised to read a signal from flag officer, U-boats, ordering *UA* to transmit beacon signals. *UA* replied with a request that the flag officer should order *U 124* to keep constant watch on the "Africa" wave, particularly as Mohr had reported the sinking of the cruiser on a wavelength that was seldom used.

Throughout December 5 we stayed more or less in the same spot, while I made provisional arrangements for the hundred men in the boats to be divided up between *UA, U 68* and *U 129*. I was determined not to wait for *U 124* after midday on December 6. However Mohr arrived after dark on the 5th, quite unaware that he had done anything wrong; he had spent a whole day chasing after the cruiser and in his opinion such an operation took priority over everything else. He had never received *UA*'s request to keep constant watch on the "Africa" wave, nor had it occurred to him to do so. He had come, he said, on the orders of the flag officer, U-boats, and now he was ready to take over his share of the survivors. I told him plainly that entirely because of his dilatoriness our men had had to spend two unnecessary nights in the lifeboats and the safety of our whole party had been jeopardized. Mohr acknowledged this reprimand with an imperturbable, "Aye, aye, sir."

Although *U 68* had little enough fuel, she handed over fifty tons to *U 129* during the night of the 6th; but this was still insufficient to get *U 129* home and she still needed to get further supplies later on. Eckermann in *UA*, who alone had plenty of fuel in reserve, refused to hand over a single ton, saying that he proposed to head for home at fourteen knots. So on the evening of December 5 *UA* and *U 129* set off homeward on separate courses; *U 68* and *U 124* sailed on the morning of the 6th. Each of the four U-boats had now got one hundred extra men on board.

Everyone knows how cramped life is on board these boats even under normal conditions. Only half the crew of fifty to sixty men can eat or sleep at the same time. We had now reached the point where room for squatting or lying down had to be reduced still further. We squatted for so many hours, we sat for so many hours and for so many hours we lay down. My eight officers shared the officer of the watch's bunk. Mohr waged an endless war with Ferry, my Scottie, who had of course been rescued with us and who always insisted on lying down just there Mohr wanted to be. There was only room for one of them on the deck and eventually they reached a compromise. Ferry lay on top of Mohr.

The U-boat's cook was naturally at his wits' end, but like all U-boat cooks he was a wizard. From a stove-plate thirty inches by fifteen built into a space no larger than a broom cupboard, he produced daily meals of goulash, macaroni and vegetables for one hundred and fifty men. We were crossing the equator now and the temperature in the U-boat stood between 96 and 100 degrees. When the boat was on the surface, only a few of us at a time could go on deck to breathe fresh air, otherwise the boat would have been unable to make a quick dive in case of an alarm.

On December 7 Slangkop radio station broadcast the British Admiralty's report of the sinking of the *Python* and added the following warning to all ships: *"It is believed that survivors from this ship, which was sunk in position 17°53'S, 3°55'W, are afloat in about fifteen boats; they may be carrying arms. They are probably close together and escorted by one or more U-boats. If sighted they should be given a wide berth and reported at once by signal."*

On December 12 our little force was ordered to rendezvous between the 13th and 17th off the Cape Verde Islands with four Italian U-boats, the *Tazzoli, Finzi, Calvi* and *Torelli,* and to hand over some of their passengers to them. Between sixty and seventy men were accordingly embarked in the Italian boats, which immediately started for home. On the way the *Torelli* ran into the escort of a Gibraltar convoy and, to cap everything after six hundred and forty days at sea, her reluctant passengers found themselves embroiled in a full-scale depth-charge attack. The U-boat arrived home, damaged, on December 23.

After a brief race with *UA, U 68* was the first to reach St. Nazaire. We arrived on Christmas Day. It was six hundred and fifty-five days since my men and I had last set foot on European soil. We had covered 110,000 miles—1,000 of them in lifeboats—and we had sunk twenty-two ships of 144,500 tons. And now we were home! For the first time a nagging load of worry was lifted from our shoulders, just as it had been on the night we had slept so peacefully beneath the shelter of the *Admiral Scheer*'s guns in the Indian Ocean.

I mustered my men by the lock gates at St. Nazaire, close to where *U 68* was berthed. Not a man among us was dressed in proper uniform—we were all wearing the most outlandish costumes. I knew that I would never forget the face of a single one of them.

The *Tazzoli* arrived on December 25, *U 129* and the *Calvi* on the 27th, the *Finzi* on the 28th and last of all *U 124* on the 29th. The whole of my ship's company was reunited at Nantes, where we stayed until New Year's Day collecting two years' arrears of mail and being fitted out with new clothing. Thanks to some superb staff work everything went forward smoothly. I held a final parade at which I took formal leave of the men who had stood by me and served under me in good days and bad, and who had survived two shipwrecks at my side; I could not help feeling very proud of them. Then I took my place at their head and we marched to church to give thanks for our safe return. I shall never forget the sound of my men's voices singing, "Now thank we all our God."

On New Year's Day, 1942, we climbed into a special train for Berlin. When the train stopped at the frontier I got out, followed by Ferry, and strolled down the platform. At one end of the station a small, leafless tree had been planted in a few inches of soil. I stopped and crumbled some of the soil in my fingers. It was damp and blackened by the frosts of winter— but it was my native soil.

There had been so many times when I had never expected to see it again.

Appendix

THE OTHER SIDE OF THE STORY

The report of the commanding officer of HMS *Devonshire* to the commander-in-chief, South Atlantic, dated November 26, 1941, was published in the *London Gazette* on July 9, 1948.

Captain R. D. Oliver, Royal Navy, reported that on November 22 his Walrus aircraft had been launched on the usual dawn reconnaissance. Since wireless silence was preserved during the flight it was only upon his return that the observer could report having sighted a merchant ship in position 4°20′S, 18°50′W. Captain Oliver's report continued: "Course was immediately altered to close this position at 25 knots. The description given contained the grounds of a suspicion that she might be a German raider. . . . The masts of a ship were sighted at 0809 . . . Wind southeast, force 4. Sky partly cloudy. Visibility ten miles. Slight sea, short slow swell.

"The Walrus was again catapulted at 0820 to carry out further investigation and for this purpose had been provided with photographs of known German raiders. The appearance of the ship closely resembled the description of Raider No. 16 given in the supplement to *Weekly Intelligence Report* No. 64 and the American magazine *Life* of June 23, 1941—with the exception of removable characteristics such as ventilators and samson posts.

"*Devonshire* was maneuvered to keep between 18,000 and 12,000 yards from the merchant ship— speed 26 knots—making frequent alterations of course to frustrate torpedo attack. . . . At 0837 *Devonshire* fired two salvoes spread to the right and left. My object was (a) to provoke a return fire and so establish her identity beyond doubt, (b) to induce her to abandon ship in order to avoid bloodshed, particularly as she might have a number of British prisoners on board. The enemy stopped and turned around and transmitted a raider report in the form '*RRR RRR RRR Polyphemus* . . .' It was noted that no signal letters were included and that three R's were transmitted in a group and not four. The possibility of the ship being in fact the *Polyphemus* had now to be considered.

"According to an Admiralty signal . . . of October 22 . . . the *Polyphemus* was at Balboa on September 21, and therefore within reach of my position. To remove what little doubt remained I signaled (to the C-in-C) '*Is Polyphemus genuine?*' and received your reply '*No repeat no.*' In the meantime a signal was passed to the aircraft '*What type of stern has she got?*' and the reply '*Cruiser stern hull similar to Atlantis*' was received at 0931.

"At 0935 *Devonshire* opened fire to destroy the enemy raider. Thirty salvoes were fired in all. The enemy turned away and started a . . . smokescreen from her stern and from both sides abreast the bridge. She also abandoned ship. No attempt was made to return my fire. Owing to the smoke I checked fire . . .

and altered course . . . to get clear of the smoke. Indirect fire by radar was attempted but proved unsuccessful. At 0943 the target was again visible and fire was re-opened, and maintained until 0956, when the ship was seen to be badly on fire forward and down by the stern . . . At 1002 her magazine blew up and it was clear that no further offensive action was necessary. . . . There was another heavy explosion at 1014 and the raider sank at 1016.

"After receiving verbal reports from the pilot and observer I had no further doubts regarding the identity of the raider and was almost certain that a U-boat had been present. Unquestionably it was impossible to rescue the survivors without grave risk of being torpedoed. . . ."

The report of Captain A. W. S. Agar, Royal Navy,

Dorsetshire

commanding HMS *Dorsetshire*, was printed in the same appendix to the *London Gazette*. According to this, while on a normal search patrol for auxiliary cruisers and U-boat supply ships, *Dorsetshire* sighted a ship's masts on Monday, December 1, close to a "relatively calm area some seven hundred and twenty miles south and west of St. Helena." As the cruiser approached the target at 25 knots for a closer inspection, it was observed that "the ship was making quite a lot of smoke and remained hull down, which confirmed my opinion that the ship was stopped when sighted and later, on sighting *Dorsetshire*, increased to full speed and altered course away from us. Speed was increased to 30 knots to close, the ship's company went to their action stations and the aircraft recalled by W/T. Small patches of oil were observed on the water, including one track which was not that of the target. These tracks all pointed to the direction in which the ship was first sighted, and gave rise at once to the suspicion that a U-boat might be in the vicinity."

Captain Agar's report continued with the description of how he sighted the *Python*'s boats with the dinghies in tow and, mistaking them at first for the conning tower of a U-boat, took evasive action; but then he realized his mistake and correctly concluded that the ship he was chasing was hostile. It also occurred to him that the fleeing ship might be a British one that had mistaken HMS *Dorsetshire* for a German warship, and that she had thus been prevented from rescuing the survivors of a ship sunk by a German U-boat.

He went on to describe how, after firing two warning shots to right and left of the target, he observed white smoke being emitted from the ship's stern, which could have been "either a smokescreen, a smokefloat dropped in the water to attract a submarine, or an explosive charge to scuttle." He therefore decided "in the circumstances to keep *Dorsetshire* moving at high speed and outside a range of eight miles so as to reduce as much as possible any risk of attack by U-boat. Within a further three minutes," he went on, "the enemy turned to starboard, stopped and commenced to lower boats. I decided to withhold fire and continued to zig-zag at high speed outside his gun and torpedo range while within ours. In this I had in mind the possibility that the enemy was a raider with British merchant seamen on board and that he should be allowed sufficient time to get the boats clear and thus save the unnecessary loss of British lives.

"At 1751 smoke commenced pouring from the bridge and foredeck, indicating she had been set on fire. This fire took hold rapidly, flames reaching the height of the funnel, with occasional minor explosions probably caused by ammunition. At 1805 she was heavily on fire when a large explosion in the forepart of the ship settled the business and she sank at 1821, leaving only a trail of smoke behind and a number of survivors in boats. . . . The enemy did not fire on *Dorsetshire* and no torpedo tracks were observed. At 18,000 yards or more she would have had little chance of doing *Dorsetshire* much damage before she herself was out of action with heavy casualties. . . . My own opinion is that the enemy was relying on U-boat protection and with the large number of men on board, decided to abandon ship at the first opportunity, hoping that *Dorsetshire* would close to pick up survivors, when perhaps an opportunity for attack by U-boat would present itself. The efficiency and speed with which she abandoned ship shows that this evolution must have been practiced frequently, as must also the arrangements for scuttling and setting fire to the ship. The large number of survivors—estimated by aircraft to be about five hundred—is significant. If she was a raider, this would account for British merchant seamen prisoners, otherwise the only explanation offered is that they were spare crews for U-boats."

BANTAM WAR BOOKS

Now there is a great new series of carefully selected books that together cover the full dramatic sweep of World War II heroism— viewed from all sides and representing all branches of armed service, whether on land, sea or in the air. All of the books are true stories of brave men and women. Most volumes are eyewitness accounts by those who fought in the conflict. Many of the books are already famous bestsellers.

Each book in this series contains a powerful fold-out full-color painting typifying the subject of the books; many have been specially commissioned. There are also specially commissioned identification illustrations of aircraft, weapons, vehicles, and other equipment, which accompany the text for greater understanding, plus specially commissioned maps and charts to explain unusual terrain, fighter plane tactics, and step-by-step progress of battles. Also included are carefully compiled indexes and bibliographies as an aid to further reading.

Here are the latest releases, all Bantam Books available wherever paperbacks are sold.

AS EAGLES SCREAMED by Donald Burgett

THE BIG SHOW by Pierre Clostermann

U-BOAT KILLER by Donald Macintyre

THE WHITE RABBIT by Bruce Marshall

THE ROAD PAST MANDALAY by John Masters

HORRIDO! by Raymond F. Toliver & Trevor J. Constable

COCKLESHELL HEROES by C. E. Lucas-Phillips

HELMET FOR MY PILLOW by Robert Leckie

THE COASTWATCHERS by Cmd. Eric A. Feldt

ESCORT COMMANDER by Terence Robertson

I FLEW FOR THE FÜHRER by Heinz Knoke

ENEMY COAST AHEAD by Guy Gibson

THE HUNDRED DAYS OF LT. MAC-HORTON by Ian MacHorton with Henry Maule

QUEEN OF THE FLAT-TOPS by Stanley Johnston

V-2 by Walter Dornberger